McGRAW-HILL READING

Spelling

Grade 4

Practice Book

McGraw-Hill School Division

New York   Farmington

CONTENTS

Grade 4/Unit 1

Grade 4/Unit 2

Justin and the Best Biscuits in the World
Syllable Patterns

Just a Dream
Words with Consonant Clusters

Leah's Pony
Words with Consonant Clusters

Baseball Saved Us
Plurals

Will Her Native Language Disappear?
Words from Social Studies

Grade 4/Unit 3

The Hatmaker's Sign
Words with /ou/ and /oi/

Pat Cummings: My Story
Words with /ü/ and /yü/

Grass Sandals: The Travels of Basho
Words with Digraphs

A Place Called Freedom
Adding -ed and -ing

Twisted Trails
Words from the Arts

Grade 4/Unit 4

Grade 4/Unit 5

GRADE 4/UNIT 6

Words with Short Vowels

Pretest Directions

Fold back the paper along the dotted line. Use the blanks to write each word as it is read aloud. When you finish the test, unfold the paper. Use the list at the right to correct any spelling mistakes. Practice the words you missed for the Posttest.

To Parents

Here are the results of your child's weekly spelling Pretest. You can help your child study for the Posttest by following these simple steps for each word on the word list:

1. Read the word to your child.

2. Have your child write the word, saying each letter as it is written.

3. Say each letter of the word as your child checks the spelling.

4. If a mistake has been made, have your child read each letter of the correctly spelled word aloud, and then repeat steps 1–3.

1. _____	1. drank
2. _____	2. rest
3. _____	3. ahead
4. _____	4. drink
5. _____	5. dock
6. _____	6. hung
7. _____	7. trouble
8. _____	8. magazines
9. _____	9. self
10. _____	10. deaf
11. _____	11. lift
12. _____	12. flock
13. _____	13. trust
14. _____	14. cousin
15. _____	15. cannon
16. _____	16. swept
17. _____	17. pleasant
18. _____	18. fist
19. _____	19. couple
20. _____	20. wealth

Challenge Words

_____ brand-new

_____ compass

_____ darted

_____ muttered

_____ talker

Name _____ **Date** _____

Words with Short Vowels

Using the Word Study Steps

1. LOOK at the word.

2. SAY the word aloud.

3. STUDY the letters in the word.

4. WRITE the word.

5. CHECK the word.

   Did you spell the word right?
   If not, go back to step 1.

Spelling Tip
Use words that you know how to spell to help you spell new words:

<u>dr</u>ip + th<u>ank</u> = drank

Word Scramble

Unscramble each set of letters to make a spelling word.

1. krind _____

2. nugh _____

3. kdoc _____

4. fles _____

5. zagmainse _____

6. krand _____

7. afde _____

8. tres _____

9. broulet _____

10. dahae _____

11. tilf _____

12. spewt _____

13. stif _____

14. cloupe _____

15. anconn _____

16. steapaln _____

17. sniocu _____

18. clofk _____

19. sturt _____

20. thalew _____

To Parents or Helpers

Using the Word Study Steps above as your child comes across any new words will help him or her learn to spell words effectively. Review the steps as you both go over this week's spelling words.

Go over the Spelling Tip with your child. Ask your child to think of words he or she knows that can help him or her spell other words on the list.

Help your child complete the spelling activity.

Words with Short Vowels

drank	dock	self	trust	pleasant
rest	hung	deaf	cousin	fist
ahead	trouble	lift	cannon	couple
drink	magazines	flock	swept	wealth

Sort each spelling word by finding the sound and spelling pattern to which it belongs. Write the word and circle the letter or letters that spell its vowel sound.

short a spelled

a

1. _____
2. _____
3. _____

short e spelled

e

4. _____
5. _____
6. _____

short e spelled

ea

7. _____
8. _____
9. _____
10. _____

short i spelled

i

11. _____
12. _____
13. _____

short o spelled

o

14. _____
15. _____

short u spelled

u

16. _____
17. _____

short u spelled

ou

18. _____
19. _____
20. _____

Sounds Alike

Write the spelling word that rhymes with each word below.

21. health _____ **22.** double _____

Words with Short Vowels

drank	dock	self	trust	pleasant
rest	hung	deaf	cousin	fist
ahead	trouble	lift	cannon	couple
drink	magazines	flock	swept	wealth

Complete each sentence with a spelling word.

1. These _____ always have funny stories I like to read.

2. Every morning, a large _____ of birds visits my bird feeder.

3. I _____ two glasses of milk this morning at breakfast.

4. A person's _____ is who they are and how they are special.

5. Last week, the students _____ pictures on the classroom walls.

6. If you are in a hurry, you can go _____ of me in line.

7. I like to _____ a glass of juice after school.

8. My _____ Bob is my Aunt Tilly's son.

9. The clown at the circus was shot from a _____.

10. He found the broom and _____ the floor.

Define It!

Write the spelling words that have the same meanings as the words or phrases below.

11. take it easy or sleep _____

14. a place to tie a boat _____

12. two of something _____

15. to raise up _____

13. not able to hear _____

16. a tightly closed hand _____

Challenge Extension: Ask students to write a "fill in the blank" sentence for each Challenge Word and then exchange papers with a partner to complete the sentences.

Words with Short Vowels

Proofreading Activity

There are six spelling mistakes in the letter below. Circle the misspelled words. Write the words correctly on the lines below.

Dear Cusin Bob,

    I had a wonderful time with my dad this summer. We hiked into the mountains. Dad hiked ahede of me because I had truble climbing. I had to stop and reast a lot. But soon we found a lake. We draink water right from the lake! Once I thought we were lost. Dad said we could troust his compass to help us find our way. And he was right. It was the best vacation I ever had.

See you soon,
Luke

1. _____ 3. _____ 5. _____

2. _____ 4. _____ 6. _____

Writing Activity

Write a letter to a friend about a holiday or vacation you once had. Use four spelling words in your writing.

_____

_____

_____

_____

Words with Short Vowels

Look at the words in each set below. One word in each set is spelled correctly. Use a pencil to fill in the circle next to the correct word. Before you begin, look at the sample sets of words. Sample A has been done for you. Do Sample B by yourself. When you are sure you know what to do, you may go on with the rest of the page.

Sample A
- Ⓐ beest
- ⬤Ⓑ best
- Ⓒ beste
- Ⓓ biest

Sample B
- Ⓔ ring
- Ⓕ ringe
- Ⓖ raing
- Ⓗ reing

1.
- Ⓐ docke
- Ⓑ dock
- Ⓒ doick
- Ⓓ dok

6.
- Ⓔ lifft
- Ⓕ lift
- Ⓖ lifte
- Ⓗ liaft

11.
- Ⓐ megizines
- Ⓑ magazines
- Ⓒ magazanes
- Ⓓ magizins

16.
- Ⓔ sweept
- Ⓕ swept
- Ⓖ swiept
- Ⓗ sweeped

2.
- Ⓔ cannin
- Ⓕ kannon
- Ⓖ cannon
- Ⓗ canin

7.
- Ⓐ silf
- Ⓑ sealf
- Ⓒ selfe
- Ⓓ self

12.
- Ⓔ deaf
- Ⓕ deef
- Ⓖ def
- Ⓗ daef

17.
- Ⓐ welth
- Ⓑ weelth
- Ⓒ walth
- Ⓓ wealth

3.
- Ⓐ drinke
- Ⓑ drienk
- Ⓒ drink
- Ⓓ drenk

8.
- Ⓔ huhng
- Ⓕ hung
- Ⓖ hunge
- Ⓗ hungh

13.
- Ⓐ truste
- Ⓑ troust
- Ⓒ trost
- Ⓓ trust

18.
- Ⓔ pleasant
- Ⓕ plesant
- Ⓖ pleasint
- Ⓗ plezant

4.
- Ⓔ trubble
- Ⓕ trouble
- Ⓖ troubel
- Ⓗ truble

9.
- Ⓐ riste
- Ⓑ rest
- Ⓒ reist
- Ⓓ reste

14.
- Ⓔ flouck
- Ⓕ flock
- Ⓖ flok
- Ⓗ flocke

19.
- Ⓐ feste
- Ⓑ fis
- Ⓒ fist
- Ⓓ fiste

5.
- Ⓐ ahead
- Ⓑ ahed
- Ⓒ ahaed
- Ⓓ ahede

10.
- Ⓔ drenk
- Ⓕ draink
- Ⓖ draenk
- Ⓗ drank

15.
- Ⓐ cousin
- Ⓑ cusin
- Ⓒ cousen
- Ⓓ cuzin

20.
- Ⓔ cuple
- Ⓕ copple
- Ⓖ cuppel
- Ⓗ couple

Words with Long *a* and Long *e*

Pretest Directions

Fold back the paper along the dotted line. Use the blanks to write each word as it is read aloud. When you finish the test, unfold the paper. Use the list at the right to correct any spelling mistakes. Practice the words you missed for the Posttest.

To Parents

Here are the results of your child's weekly spelling Pretest. You can help your child study for the Posttest by following these simple steps for each word on the word list:

1. Read the word to your child.

2. Have your child write the word, saying each letter as it is written.

3. Say each letter of the word as your child checks the spelling.

4. If a mistake has been made, have your child read each letter of the correctly spelled word aloud, then repeat steps 1–3.

1. _____	1. cape
2. _____	2. gray
3. _____	3. station
4. _____	4. rail
5. _____	5. freight
6. _____	6. agree
7. _____	7. teacher
8. _____	8. secret
9. _____	9. family
10. _____	10. cane
11. _____	11. crayon
12. _____	12. cable
13. _____	13. fail
14. _____	14. tea
15. _____	15. zebra
16. _____	16. rusty
17. _____	17. tray
18. _____	18. raisin
19. _____	19. bean
20. _____	20. tidy

Challenge Words

_____ accidental

_____ labored

_____ occasions

_____ rhythms

_____ shutters

Name_____ **Date**_____

Words with Long *a* and Long *e*

Using the Word Study Steps

1. LOOK at the word.
2. SAY the word aloud.
3. STUDY the letters in the word.
4. WRITE the word.
5. CHECK the word.

   Did you spell the word right?
   If not, go back to step 1.

Spelling Tip

Use words that you know how to spell to help you spell new words.

fr + eight = freight

Word Scramble

Unscramble each set of letters to make a spelling word.

1. greae _____
2. lira _____
3. giefrth _____
4. epac _____
5. rehatec _____
6. nace _____
7. maliyf _____
8. yrag _____
9. creets _____
10. sattnoi _____

11. tsury _____
12. eat _____
13. neab _____
14. diyt _____
15. rabez _____
16. ialf _____
17. yarcno _____
18. siainr _____
19. lebac _____
20. yart _____

To Parents or Helpers

   Using the Word Study Steps above as your child comes across any new words will help him or her learn to spell words effectively. Review the steps as you both go over this week's spelling words.
   Go over the Spelling Tip with your child. Ask your child to look at the spelling words and see if any of them contain smaller words that he or she knows how to spell.
   Help your child complete the word scramble.

Words with Long a and Long e

cape	freight	family	fail	tray
gray	agree	cane	tea	raisin
station	teacher	crayon	zebra	bean
rail	secret	cable	rusty	tidy

Pattern Power!

Sort each spelling word by finding the sound and spelling pattern to which it belongs. Write the word and circle the letter or letters that spell its vowel sound.

Long *a* spelled

ae

1. _____

2. _____

ay

3. _____

4. _____

5. _____

ai

6. _____

7. _____

8. _____

a

9. _____

10. _____

eigh

11. _____

Long *e* spelled

ee

12. _____

ea

13. _____

14. _____

15. _____

e

16. _____

17. _____

y

18. _____

19. _____

20. _____

Words with Long *a* and Long *e*

cape	freight	family	fail	tray
gray	agree	cane	tea	raisin
station	teacher	crayon	zebra	bean
rail	secret	cable	rusty	tidy

Complete each sentence below with a spelling word.

1. The bus _____ is five miles from my house.

2. That _____ train carries food to the city.

3. If I mix white and black together, I will have the color _____.

4. It is not a _____ that she loves to dance.

5. Do you disagree, or _____ with me?

6. The new _____ wrote her name on the chalkboard.

7. The dented metal looks red and _____.

8. I will carry the cookies to the children on a _____.

9. Use a _____ to color in your coloring book.

10. The newest, fastest trains run on only one _____.

What Does it Mean?
Write the spelling word that has the same, or almost the same meaning.

11. flunk _____

12. neat _____

13. relatives _____

14. striped animal _____

15. seed of a plant _____

16. a dried fruit _____

17. hot drink _____

18. walking stick _____

Challenge Extension: Have students create Challenge Word scrambles. Then have students swap them with a partner and solve each other's word scramble.

Words with Long *a* and Long *e*

Proofreading Activity

There are six spelling mistakes in the letter below. Circle the misspelled words. Write the words correctly on the lines below.

Dear Mrs. Ramos,

    Thank you for being so nice to me. I want to tell you a seecret. Even though my family had to move to find work, I will come back to see you. I hope to build a small, tiedy house near the big tree. I will live there forever with my pretty, grae cat, Kitty. When I move into my wonderful house, I will not fale to come and see you. You are the best teecher I ever had.

Your student,
Amelia

1. _____ 3. _____ 5. _____

2. _____ 4. _____ 6. _____

Writing Activity

Where would you like to live? Write a letter telling a friend what your place will look like. Use four spelling words in your writing.

_____

_____

_____

_____

Words with Long *a* and Long *e*

Look at the words in each set below. One word in each set is spelled correctly. Use a pencil to fill in the circle next to the correct word. Before you begin, look at the sample sets of words. Sample A has been done for you. Do Sample B by yourself. When you are sure you know what to do, you may go on with the rest of the page.

Sample A
Ⓐ ranne
Ⓑ rane
Ⓒ rain
Ⓓ raine

Sample B
Ⓔ nete
Ⓕ neat
Ⓖ neit
Ⓗ neate

1.
Ⓐ teye
Ⓑ tea
Ⓒ tei
Ⓓ tae

2.
Ⓔ cane
Ⓕ cain
Ⓖ caine
Ⓗ ceane

3.
Ⓐ ugree
Ⓑ agrey
Ⓒ aggre
Ⓓ agree

4.
Ⓔ rason
Ⓕ raisin
Ⓖ raesin
Ⓗ raysin

5.
Ⓐ tidee
Ⓑ tyde
Ⓒ tidi
Ⓓ tidy

6.
Ⓔ crayon
Ⓕ craiyon
Ⓖ crayen
Ⓗ craon

7.
Ⓐ zibra
Ⓑ zebra
Ⓒ zeebra
Ⓓ zeabra

8.
Ⓔ capp
Ⓕ cape
Ⓖ caip
Ⓗ caipe

9.
Ⓐ station
Ⓑ staytion
Ⓒ stashun
Ⓓ steation

10.
Ⓔ trai
Ⓕ traye
Ⓖ tray
Ⓗ trei

11.
Ⓐ famile
Ⓑ family
Ⓒ familee
Ⓓ famely

12.
Ⓔ rale
Ⓕ rael
Ⓖ raile
Ⓗ rail

13.
Ⓐ teecher
Ⓑ teachur
Ⓒ teacher
Ⓓ taecher

14.
Ⓔ gray
Ⓕ grei
Ⓖ grai
Ⓗ graye

15.
Ⓐ frate
Ⓑ freight
Ⓒ freite
Ⓓ freaght

16.
Ⓔ cayble
Ⓕ caible
Ⓖ cable
Ⓗ cabl

17.
Ⓐ bean
Ⓑ beene
Ⓒ beane
Ⓓ bene

18.
Ⓔ seecret
Ⓕ secrete
Ⓖ seicret
Ⓗ secret

19.
Ⓐ rousty
Ⓑ rusty
Ⓒ ruste
Ⓓ rustey

20.
Ⓔ fale
Ⓕ faile
Ⓖ fayle
Ⓗ fail

Words with Long *i* and Long *o*

Pretest Directions

Fold back the paper along the dotted line. Use the blanks to write each word as it is read aloud. When you finish the test, unfold the paper. Use the list at the right to correct any spelling mistakes. Practice the words you missed for the Posttest.

To Parents

Here are the results of your child's weekly spelling Pretest. You can help your child study for the Posttest by following these simple steps for each word on the word list:

1. Read the word to your child.

2. Have your child write the word, saying each letter as it is written.

3. Say each letter of the word as your child checks the spelling.

4. If a mistake has been made, have your child read each letter of the correctly spelled word aloud, then repeat steps 1–3.

1. _____	1. tiger
2. _____	2. drive
3. _____	3. reply
4. _____	4. roll
5. _____	5. note
6. _____	6. crow
7. _____	7. oak
8. _____	8. iron
9. _____	9. alike
10. _____	10. supply
11. _____	11. tomato
12. _____	12. stove
13. _____	13. below
14. _____	14. groan
15. _____	15. title
16. _____	16. pine
17. _____	17. overhead
18. _____	18. chose
19. _____	19. hollow
20. _____	20. file

Challenge Words

_____	eerie
_____	huddled
_____	pesky
_____	reins
_____	squall

Words with Long *i* and Long *o*

Using the Word Study Steps

1. LOOK at the word.
2. SAY the word aloud.
3. STUDY the letters in the word.
4. WRITE the word.
5. CHECK the word.

   Did you spell the word right?
   If not, go back to step 1.

Spelling Tip

Think of a word you know that has the same spelling pattern as the word you want to spell, such as a rhyming word.

sn<u>ow</u>   r<u>ow</u>   cr<u>ow</u>

Find Rhyming Words

Circle the word in each row that rhymes with the spelling word in dark type.

1. **drive**	alive	brave
2. **crow**	claw	grow
3. **pine**	shine	pain
4. **alike**	stick	strike
5. **oak**	soak	bark
6. **below**	now	throw
7. **file**	fail	mile

8. **supply**	supper	fly
9. **groan**	spoon	loan
10. **note**	not	wrote
11. **tomato**	too	potato
12. **stove**	drove	move
13. **overhead**	bead	dead
14. **chose**	those	choose

Word Unscramble

Unscramble each set of letters to make a spelling word.

15. loowlh   _____

16. griet   _____

17. rino   _____

18. lolr   _____

19. litte   _____

20. pyrle   _____

To Parents or Helpers

Using the Word Study Steps above as your child comes across any new words will help him or her learn to spell words effectively. Review the steps as you both go over this week's spelling words.

Go over the Spelling Tip with your child. Ask your child if he or she can think of any words that rhyme with one of the spelling words. Help your child complete the spelling activity

EXPORE THE PATTERN

Words with Long i and Long o

tiger	note	alike	below	overhead
drive	crow	supply	groan	chose
reply	oak	tomato	title	hollow
roll	iron	stove	pine	file

Write the spelling words with these spelling patterns.

Long *i* spelled

i-e

1. _____
2. _____
3. _____
4. _____

i

5. _____
6. _____
7. _____

y

8. _____
9. _____

Long *o* spelled

o

10. _____
11. _____
12. _____

o-e

13. _____
14. _____
15. _____

ow

16. _____
17. _____
18. _____

oa

19. _____
20. _____

Words with Long *i* and Long *o*

tiger	note	alike	below	overhead
drive	crow	supply	groan	chose
reply	oak	tomato	title	hollow
roll	iron	stove	pine	file

Complete each sentence below with a spelling word.

1. If your shirt gets wrinkled, you can use my _____.

2. When I grow up, my mom will teach me to _____ a car.

3. A large black _____ flew into the clouds.

4. The _____ of this story is <u>Sarah, Plain and Tall</u>.

5. The _____ took a nap in its cage at the zoo.

6. Mom used the top of our _____ to fry onions.

7. Acorns are seeds from big _____ trees.

8. At the office, all papers are kept in a _____.

9. A _____ tree has long, thin needles for leaves.

10. I keep a large _____ of dog food in the house.

What Does it Mean?
Write the spelling word that has the same, or almost the same, meaning.

11. empty _____ **15.** under _____

12. answer _____ **16.** above _____

13. picked out _____ **17.** moan _____

14. the same or similar _____ **18.** letter _____

Challenge Extension: Have students write fill-in sentences for each Challenge Word. Have each student exchange sentences with a partner and fill each other's sentences.

Words with Long *i* and Long *o*

Proofreading Activity

There are six spelling mistakes in the paragraph below. Circle the misspelled words. Write the words correctly on the lines below.

Sarah just got back from town. She brought us a suply of food for dinner. She cooked rich, delicious tomado soup on the stoov. Then she made us warm, brown dinner rowls. We ate outside, in the shade of the huge, old oke tree. Overhed, the birds sang to each other in the branches. It was a wonderful day, and I was very happy.

1. _____ 3. _____ 5. _____

2. _____ 4. _____ 6. _____

Writing Activity

Sarah liked to drive to town. Write a short story about a drive you would like to take. Use four spelling words in your writing.

_____

_____

_____

_____

Words with Long *i* and Long *o*

Look at the words in each set below. One word in each set is spelled correctly. Use a pencil to fill in the circle next to the correct word. Before you begin, look at the sample sets of words. Sample A has been done for you. Do Sample B by yourself. When you are sure you know what to do, you may go on with the rest of the page.

Sample A
- Ⓐ groo
- 🅑 grow
- Ⓒ groe
- Ⓓ groh

Sample B
- Ⓔ vote
- Ⓕ vot
- Ⓖ voat
- Ⓗ voot

1.
- Ⓐ driv
- Ⓑ drive
- Ⓒ driev
- Ⓓ dryve

2.
- Ⓔ crow
- Ⓕ craw
- Ⓖ croe
- Ⓗ croo

3.
- Ⓐ pyn
- Ⓑ pihn
- Ⓒ pien
- Ⓓ pine

4.
- Ⓔ alick
- Ⓕ aliek
- Ⓖ alike
- Ⓗ alik

5.
- Ⓐ oke
- Ⓑ oak
- Ⓒ ok
- Ⓓ oek

6.
- Ⓔ below
- Ⓕ bilow
- Ⓖ beloe
- Ⓗ beloo

7.
- Ⓐ fil
- Ⓑ file
- Ⓒ fiel
- Ⓓ fyel

8.
- Ⓔ supplie
- Ⓕ suply
- Ⓖ suppley
- Ⓗ supply

9.
- Ⓐ grone
- Ⓑ groen
- Ⓒ groan
- Ⓓ graon

10.
- Ⓔ nowt
- Ⓕ noot
- Ⓖ noet
- Ⓗ note

11.
- Ⓐ tomado
- Ⓑ tomato
- Ⓒ toomatoe
- Ⓓ tomatoe

12.
- Ⓔ stoove
- Ⓕ stov
- Ⓖ stove
- Ⓗ stohve

13.
- Ⓐ overhead
- Ⓑ ovuhead
- Ⓒ overhed
- Ⓓ overhad

14.
- Ⓔ choos
- Ⓕ chose
- Ⓖ chois
- Ⓗ choss

15.
- Ⓐ hollo
- Ⓑ holluh
- Ⓒ holloh
- Ⓓ hollow

16.
- Ⓔ tiger
- Ⓕ tiegr
- Ⓖ tyger
- Ⓗ tigger

17.
- Ⓐ iorn
- Ⓑ iyern
- Ⓒ iron
- Ⓓ iern

18.
- Ⓔ rol
- Ⓕ roll
- Ⓖ rool
- Ⓗ rowl

19.
- Ⓐ tiltell
- Ⓑ titel
- Ⓒ tietl
- Ⓓ title

20.
- Ⓔ repliye
- Ⓕ reply
- Ⓖ replie
- Ⓗ repli

Words with /ū/ and /ü/

Pretest Directions
Fold back the paper along the dotted line. Use the blanks to write each word as it is read aloud. When you finish the test, unfold the paper. Use the list at the right to correct any spelling mistakes. Practice the words you missed for the Posttest.

To Parents
Here are the results of your child's weekly spelling Pretest. You can help your child study for the Posttest by following these simple steps for each word on the word list:

1. Read the word to your child.

2. Have your child write the word, saying each letter as it is written.

3. Say each letter of the word as your child checks the spelling.

4. If a mistake has been made, have your child read each letter of the correctly spelled word aloud, then repeat steps 1–3.

1. _____ 1. ruler
2. _____ 2. avenue
3. _____ 3. raccoon
4. _____ 4. loose
5. _____ 5. commute
6. _____ 6. continue
7. _____ 7. gloomy
8. _____ 8. unit
9. _____ 9. whose
10. _____ 10. humor
11. _____ 11. improve
12. _____ 12. beautiful
13. _____ 13. cube
14. _____ 14. stool
15. _____ 15. movement
16. _____ 16. ruin
17. _____ 17. bugle
18. _____ 18. argue
19. _____ 19. community
20. _____ 20. tuna

Challenge Words

_____ assured
_____ horizon
_____ jagged
_____ mature
_____ squealed

Words with /ū/ and /ü/

Using the Word Study Steps

1. LOOK at the word.

2. SAY the word aloud.

3. STUDY the letters in the word.

4. WRITE the word.

5. CHECK the word.

   Did you spell the word right?
   If not, go back to step 1.

Spelling Tip

Keep an Alphabetical Personal Word List Notebook. Write words you often have trouble spelling.

Find and Circle

Where are the spelling words?

```
a a x x c o m m u t e x x g l o o m y a a b u n i t x v a v e n u e

a b r u l e r x x l o o s e y y z c o n t i n u e z z r a c c o o n a b z

s t o o l a b x x c u b e z z m o v e m e n t z z r u i n a b z z x x

a a w h o s e g x h u m o r z z b e a u t i f u l c c o m m u n i t y

x x b u g l e v v i m p r o v e y y a r g u e a b b c t u n a x y z z
```

To Parents or Helpers

     Using the Word Study Steps above as your child comes across any new words will help him or her learn to spell words effectively. Review the steps as you both go over this week's spelling words.

     Go over the Spelling Tip with your child. Ask him or her if he or she can think of words that are difficult to spell. Invite him or her to write it in a notebook.

     Help your child find and circle the spelling words in the puzzle.

Words with /ū/ and /ü/

ruler	commute	whose	cube	bugle
avenue	continue	humor	stool	argue
raccoon	gloomy	improve	movement	community
loose	unit	beautiful	ruin	tuna

Write each spelling words under the spelling pattern to which it belongs and circle the spelling pattern letter or letters.

/ū/ spelled
u

1. _____
2. _____
3. _____
4. _____

/ū/ spelled
u-e

5. _____
6. _____

/ū/ spelled
ue

7. _____
8. _____
9. _____

/ū/ spelled
eau

10. _____

/ü/ spelled
u

11. _____
12. _____
13. _____

/ü/ spelled
oo

14. _____
15. _____
16. _____
17. _____

/ü/ spelled
o-e

18. _____
19. _____
20. _____

Words with /ū/ and /ü/

ruler	commute	whose	cube	bugle
avenue	continue	humor	stool	argue
raccoon	gloomy	improve	movement	community
loose	unit	beautiful	ruin	tuna

Complete each sentence below with a spelling word or words.

1. A king is the _____ of a country.

2. I play the _____ in the school marching band.

3. She knows _____ books these are.

4. The _____ sat on the tree branch and looked at me.

5. If I _____ to practice, I may make the baseball team.

6. The people who live in my _____ are very friendly.

7. Put a leash on the dog, or he will get _____.

8. Many people _____ to work by train.

9. The nursery is just one _____ in the hospital.

10. He put an ice _____ in his drink.

11. A joke with good _____ can make you laugh.

12. The child stepped up on the _____ to reach the sink.

Synonym Alert!

Write the spelling word that has the same, or almost the same, meaning.

1. road   _____   5. pretty   _____

2. dark or sad   _____   6. destroy   _____

3. disagree or fight   _____   7. make better   _____

4. motion   _____   8. fish   _____

22

Challenge Extension: Have students write one
sentence for each Challenge Word.

Grade 4/Unit 1
Seal Journey 20

Name_____ Date_____ **Spelling** **23**

Words with /ū/ and /ü/

Proofreading Activity

There are six spelling mistakes in the paragraph below. Circle the misspelled words. Write the words correctly on the lines below.

    The baby seal looked like a bootiful white ball of fur. It made a muvment toward its mother. Its mother will continu to feed it milk for twelve days. Seals eat small fish and shrimp, not big fish, like the toona. Soon the whole communeity of seals will swim north. It makes me sad and glumy, to say goodbye to the baby seals.

1. _____   3. _____   5. _____

2. _____   4. _____   6. _____

Writing Activity

Think about an adventure you would like. Where would you go and what would you do? Write a paragraph using four spelling words in your writing.

_____

_____

_____

_____

Words with /ū/ and /ü/

Look at the words in each set below. One word in each set is spelled correctly. Use a pencil to fill in the circle next to the correct word. Before you begin, look at the sample sets of words. Sample A has been done for you. Do Sample B by yourself. When you are sure you know what to do, you may go on with the rest of the page.

Sample A
- Ⓐ ceaut
- Ⓑ cuet
- Ⓒ cutt
- ⬤ cute

Sample B
- Ⓔ bute
- Ⓕ boot
- Ⓖ bote
- Ⓗ byte

1.
- Ⓐ unet
- Ⓑ unitt
- Ⓒ unit
- Ⓓ unyt

2.
- Ⓔ commute
- Ⓕ comute
- Ⓖ commut
- Ⓗ commoot

3.
- Ⓐ avenoo
- Ⓑ avenue
- Ⓒ avenu
- Ⓓ avenoe

4.
- Ⓔ ruler
- Ⓕ rooler
- Ⓖ rular
- Ⓗ ruller

5.
- Ⓐ byootiful
- Ⓑ beatiful
- Ⓒ beutiful
- Ⓓ beautiful

6.
- Ⓔ loos
- Ⓕ loose
- Ⓖ luose
- Ⓗ looce

7.
- Ⓐ woos
- Ⓑ whos
- Ⓒ whose
- Ⓓ whooz

8.
- Ⓔ humor
- Ⓕ hoomor
- Ⓖ humur
- Ⓗ heumor

9.
- Ⓐ kube
- Ⓑ cyube
- Ⓒ cube
- Ⓓ coobe

10.
- Ⓔ continu
- Ⓕ continyu
- Ⓖ continooe
- Ⓗ continue

11.
- Ⓐ rooin
- Ⓑ ruine
- Ⓒ ruin
- Ⓓ ruen

12.
- Ⓔ raccune
- Ⓕ raccoon
- Ⓖ raccun
- Ⓗ raccoun

13.
- Ⓐ improv
- Ⓑ improov
- Ⓒ improove
- Ⓓ improve

14.
- Ⓔ glumy
- Ⓕ gloomie
- Ⓖ gloomy
- Ⓗ gloomey

15.
- Ⓐ tuna
- Ⓑ tuona
- Ⓒ toona
- Ⓓ tunae

16.
- Ⓔ byugle
- Ⓕ boogle
- Ⓖ bugel
- Ⓗ bugle

17.
- Ⓐ stuol
- Ⓑ stoole
- Ⓒ stool
- Ⓓ stoul

18.
- Ⓔ movement
- Ⓕ movment
- Ⓖ moovement
- Ⓗ muvement

19.
- Ⓐ comyunity
- Ⓑ community
- Ⓒ comoonity
- Ⓓ comunity

20.
- Ⓔ argoo
- Ⓕ argyue
- Ⓖ argue
- Ⓗ argu

Words from Health

Fold back the paper along the dotted line. Use the blanks to write each word as it is read aloud. When you finish the test, unfold the paper. Use the list at the right to correct any spelling mistakes. Practice the words that you missed for the Posttest.

To Parents
Here are the results of your child's weekly spelling Pretest. You can help your child study for the Posttest by following these simple steps for each word on the list:

1. Read the word to your child.

2. Have your child write the word, saying each letter as it is written.

3. Say each letter of the word as your child checks the spelling.

4. If a mistake has been made, have your child read each letter of the correctly spelled word aloud, then repeat steps 1–3.

1. _____
2. _____
3. _____
4. _____
5. _____
6. _____
7. _____
8. _____
9. _____
10. _____
11. _____
12. _____
13. _____
14. _____
15. _____
16. _____
17. _____
18. _____
19. _____
20. _____

1. dentist
2. crown
3. hospital
4. medicine
5. diet
6. gums
7. gland
8. joint
9. fever
10. chewing
11. brain
12. cavity
13. disease
14. plaque
15. vitamin
16. ache
17. dental
18. clinic
19. oral
20. molars

Challenge Words

_____
_____
_____
_____
_____

fangs
patients
healthy
reptiles
skills

Words from Health

Using the Word Study Steps

1. LOOK at the word.

2. SAY the word aloud.

3. STUDY the letters in the word.

4. WRITE the word.

5. CHECK the word.

    Did you spell the word right?
    If not, go back to step 1.

Spelling Tip

Keep an Alphabetical Personal Word List Notebook. Write words you often have trouble spelling.

Word Scramble

Unscramble each set of letters to make a spelling word.

1. wronc _____

2. tojin _____

3. whignec _____

4. inbar _____

5. splohati _____

6. iedt _____

7. edesias _____

8. niccil _____

9. nimtaiv _____

10. ndagl _____

11. stentid _____

12. vityca _____

13. mugs _____

14. slarom _____

15. heac _____

16. refev _____

17. nideicem _____

18. loar _____

19. ledant _____

20. qlaupe _____

To Parents or Helpers

   Using the Word Study Steps above as your child comes across any new words will help him or her learn to spell words effectively. Review the steps as you both go over this week's spelling words.

   Go over the Spelling Tip with your child. Help him or her spell new words by practicing words written in a Personal Word List.

   Help your child complete the spelling activity.

Words from Health

dentist	diet	fever	disease	dental
crown	gums	chewing	plaque	clinic
hospital	gland	brain	vitamin	oral
medicine	joint	cavity	ache	molars

Word Sort
Write the spelling words with these spelling patterns.

one syllable

1. _____ 2. _____ 3. _____

4. _____ 5. _____ 6. _____

7. _____

two syllables

8. _____ 9. _____ 10. _____

11. _____ 12. _____ 13. _____

14. _____ 15. _____ 16. _____

three syllables

17. _____ 18. _____ 19. _____

20. _____

Rhyme Time
Write the spelling word that rhymes with each word below.

1. plane _____ 4. take _____

2. mental _____ 5. sand _____

3. track _____ 6. gravity _____

Words from Health

dentist	diet	fever	disease	dental
crown	gums	chewing	plaque	clinic
hospital	gland	brain	vitamin	oral
medicine	joint	cavity	ache	molars

Part of the Group
Read the heading for each group of words. Then add the spelling word that belongs in each pair.

Parts of the Mouth

1. tongue, _____

2. teeth, _____

Tooth Problems

3. pain, _____

4. stains, _____

5. hole, _____

Other Parts of the Body

6. head, _____

7. bone, _____

Where to Go for Help

8. doctor, _____

9. office, _____

10. emergency room, _____

What Does it Mean?
Write the spelling word that matches the meanings below.

11. having to do with teeth

_____

12. what you eat and drink

_____

13. having to do with the mouth

_____

14. an artificial tooth part

_____

15. grinding food with teeth

_____

16. a harmful condition

_____

17. a high body temperature

_____

18. produces saliva

_____

19. drug to relieve pain

_____

20. healthful part of foods

_____

Challenge Extension: Imagine you visit the office of an animal doctor. Write one sentence for each Challenge Word describing your visit.

28

Grade 4/Unit 1
Open Wide, Don't Bite 20

Words from Health

Proofreading Activity

There are six spelling mistakes in the paragraph below. Circle the misspelled words. Write the words correctly on the lines below.

How do you know if a tiger has a tooth acke? Well, it may stop chooing and eating. It may have a feevr. Then it is time to call the animal dentest, who will fix the tooth. Maybe the tiger has a cavty that needs to be filled. Maybe the tiger needs medecene to get better. Keepers at the zoo will make sure the tiger gets well.

1. _____ 3. _____ 5. _____

2. _____ 4. _____ 6. _____

Writing Activity

Pretend you are an animal dentist. Write a dental report about an animal whose teeth you just fixed. Use four spelling words in your writing.

_____

_____

_____

_____

Words from Health

Look at the words in each set below. One word in each set is spelled correctly. Use a pencil to fill in the circle next to the correct word. Before you begin, look at the sample sets of words. Sample A has been done for you. Do Sample B by yourself. When you are sure you know what to do, you may go on with the rest of the page.

Sample A
- (A) harte
- (B) hert
- (C) heart ●
- (D) haert

Sample B
- (E) mouth
- (F) mout
- (G) mooth
- (H) mouthe

1.
- (A) dintest
- (B) dentist
- (C) dentest
- (D) dintist

6.
- (E) gumz
- (F) gams
- (G) gums
- (H) gims

11.
- (A) brane
- (B) braine
- (C) brain
- (D) brean

16.
- (E) ake
- (F) ache
- (G) ach
- (H) eake

2.
- (E) crown
- (F) cruhn
- (G) croun
- (H) crowm

7.
- (A) gland
- (B) glend
- (C) glaind
- (D) glande

12.
- (E) cavity
- (F) cavty
- (G) kavity
- (H) cavitty

17.
- (A) dental
- (B) dintul
- (C) dentul
- (D) dantal

3.
- (A) haspitul
- (B) hahspital
- (C) hospitul
- (D) hospital

8.
- (E) jownt
- (F) joynt
- (G) joint
- (H) joent

13.
- (A) desease
- (B) diseez
- (C) disease
- (D) deseas

18.
- (E) clinq
- (F) clinyc
- (G) clinick
- (H) clinic

4.
- (E) medsin
- (F) medisin
- (G) medecin
- (H) medicine

9.
- (A) fevr
- (B) feever
- (C) fiever
- (D) fever

14.
- (E) plake
- (F) plack
- (G) plaq
- (H) plaque

19.
- (A) orul
- (B) oral
- (C) orral
- (D) aurol

5.
- (A) dyet
- (B) diet
- (C) dyit
- (D) deit

10.
- (E) chooing
- (F) chewing
- (G) chawing
- (H) cheuwing

15.
- (A) vitmin
- (B) vytamin
- (C) vitamin
- (D) vitimin

20.
- (E) molrs
- (F) moolars
- (G) molars
- (H) molers

Grade 4/Unit 1 Review Test

Read each sentence. If an underlined word is spelled wrong, fill in the circle that goes with that word. If no word is spelled wrong, fill in the circle below NONE. Read Sample A, and do Sample B.

A. We arrived at the <u>docke</u> <u>ahead</u> of the <u>rest</u>.
     A   B   C

A. (Ⓐ) Ⓑ Ⓒ Ⓓ NONE

B. They <u>chose</u> to <u>continue</u> their <u>drive</u> in the country.
      E   F   G

B. Ⓔ Ⓕ Ⓖ Ⓗ NONE

1. He <u>drank</u> a <u>cuple</u> of cans of <u>tomato</u> juice.
      A   B   C

1. Ⓐ Ⓑ Ⓒ Ⓓ NONE

2. He used his <u>wealth</u> to fix the <u>rusty</u> <u>frate</u> train.
              E   F   G

2. Ⓔ Ⓕ Ⓖ Ⓗ NONE

3. She held the <u>craeyon</u> in her <u>fist</u> and drew a <u>zebra</u>.
               A   B   C

3. Ⓐ Ⓑ Ⓒ Ⓓ NONE

4. Did he <u>grone</u> when he saw the <u>wealth</u> of <u>plaque</u>?
         E   F   G

4. Ⓔ Ⓕ Ⓖ Ⓗ NONE

5. The bus <u>movment</u> up the <u>avenue</u> slowed our <u>commute</u>.
            A   B   C

5. Ⓐ Ⓑ Ⓒ Ⓓ NONE

6. She saw a <u>racoon</u>, a <u>zebra</u>, and a <u>flock</u> of birds.
             E   F   G

6. Ⓔ Ⓕ Ⓖ Ⓗ NONE

7. The <u>couple</u> <u>drank</u> milk and ate <u>raisin</u> bread.
         A   B   C

7. Ⓐ Ⓑ Ⓒ Ⓓ NONE

8. The <u>freight</u> train held a <u>suply</u> of coal <u>below</u> the engine.
         E   F   G

8. Ⓔ Ⓕ Ⓖ Ⓗ NONE

9. A <u>vitamin</u> or a <u>medicine</u> might reduce the <u>feaver</u>.
       A   B   C

9. Ⓐ Ⓑ Ⓒ Ⓓ NONE

10. The <u>diet</u> for a <u>raccoon</u> is not the same as for a <u>zebra</u>.
          E   F   G

10. Ⓔ Ⓕ Ⓖ Ⓗ NONE

11. I found no <u>humor</u> in the slow <u>movement</u> of the <u>comute</u>.
              A   B   C

11. Ⓐ Ⓑ Ⓒ Ⓓ NONE

Go on

Grade 4 Unit 1 Review Test

12. He gave the <u>raccoon</u> some <u>medisin</u> to reduce its <u>fever</u>.
            E   F   G
12. Ⓔ Ⓕ Ⓖ Ⓗ NONE

13. A man with <u>humor</u> shared my <u>commute</u> up the <u>avenue</u>.
               A   B   C
13. Ⓐ Ⓑ Ⓒ Ⓓ NONE

14. The <u>couple</u> had a <u>tytle</u> added to the <u>plaque</u>.
        E   F   G
14. Ⓔ Ⓕ Ⓖ Ⓗ NONE

15. I am on a <u>raizin</u> and <u>tomato</u> <u>diet</u>.
            A   B   C
15. Ⓐ Ⓑ Ⓒ Ⓓ NONE

16. The <u>fever</u> caused the lady to <u>groan</u> and make a <u>fiste</u>.
        E   F   G
16. Ⓔ Ⓕ Ⓖ Ⓗ NONE

17. She held a <u>rusty</u> nail and a <u>crayon</u> in her <u>fist</u>.
             A   B   C
17. Ⓐ Ⓑ Ⓒ Ⓓ NONE

18. This <u>raisin</u> will <u>supply</u> you with a <u>vitamen</u>.
         E   F   G
18. Ⓔ Ⓕ Ⓖ Ⓗ NONE

19. I saw the <u>movement</u> of the <u>flock</u> down the <u>avenu</u>.
             A   B   C
19. Ⓐ Ⓑ Ⓒ Ⓓ NONE

20. This book's <u>title</u> is "<u>Wealth</u> and <u>Humer</u>."
            E   F   G
20. Ⓔ Ⓕ Ⓖ Ⓗ NONE

21. He <u>drank</u> juice and took a <u>vitamin</u> during his <u>dyet</u>.
         A   B   C
21. Ⓐ Ⓑ Ⓒ Ⓓ NONE

22. We heard a <u>rustie</u> wheel <u>groan</u> in the street <u>below</u>.
            E   F   G
22. Ⓔ Ⓕ Ⓖ Ⓗ NONE

23. The <u>freight</u> train carried a <u>supply</u> of <u>medicine</u>.
        A   B   C
23. Ⓐ Ⓑ Ⓒ Ⓓ NONE

24. The <u>plaque</u> had a <u>title</u> that said "Best <u>Tomatoe</u>."
        E   F   G
24. Ⓔ Ⓕ Ⓖ Ⓗ NONE

25. The <u>freight</u> train ran <u>beloew</u> the <u>flock</u> of birds.
        A   B   C
25. Ⓐ Ⓑ Ⓒ Ⓓ NONE

Syllable Patterns

Pretest Directions

Fold back the paper along the dotted line. Use the blanks to write each word as it is read aloud. When you finish the test, unfold the paper. Use the list at the right to correct any spelling mistakes. Practice the words you missed for the Posttest.

To Parents

Here are the results of your child's weekly spelling Pretest. You can help your child study for the Posttest by following these simple steps for each word on the word list:

1. Read the word to your child.

2. Have your child write the word, saying each letter as it is written.

3. Say each letter of the word as your child checks the spelling.

4. If a mistake has been made, have your child read each letter of the correctly spelled word aloud, and then repeat steps 1–3.

1. _____	1. biscuit
2. _____	2. clover
3. _____	3. public
4. _____	4. oven
5. _____	5. bandage
6. _____	6. cabin
7. _____	7. plastic
8. _____	8. radar
9. _____	9. mitten
10. _____	10. knapsack
11. _____	11. local
12. _____	12. mustard
13. _____	13. pupil
14. _____	14. sofa
15. _____	15. welcome
16. _____	16. razor
17. _____	17. fancy
18. _____	18. limit
19. _____	19. famous
20. _____	20. item

Challenge Words

_____	festival
_____	guilt
_____	inspecting
_____	lingered
_____	resounded

Name_____ Date_____

Syllable Patterns

Using the Word Study Steps

1. LOOK at the word.

2. SAY the word aloud.

3. STUDY the letters in the word.

4. WRITE the word.

5. CHECK the word.

   Did you spell the word right? If not, go back to step 1.

Spelling Tip
Look for word chunks or smaller words that can help you remember the spelling of a word. Do you see the words *band* and *age* in *bandage*?

Word Scramble

Unscramble each set of letters to make a spelling word.

1. emit _____

2. timil _____

3. orzar _____

4. faso _____

5. dratsum _____

6. sankpack _____

7. darra _____

8. binca _____

9. vone _____

10. volcer _____

11. clipbu _____

12. badgean _____

13. cutisbi _____

14. clapsit _____

15. tentim _____

16. colla _____

17. lippu _____

18. cowmele _____

19. canfy _____

20. amusfo _____

To Parents or Helpers

Using the Word Study Steps above as your child comes across any new words will help him or her learn to spell words effectively. Review the steps as you both go over this week's spelling words.

Go over the Spelling Tip with your child. Help your child find chunks or smaller words in the spelling words to help remember how to spell them.

Help your child complete the spelling activity.

Syllable Patterns

biscuit	bandage	mitten	pupil	fancy
clover	cabin	knapsack	sofa	limit
public	plastic	local	welcome	famous
oven	radar	mustard	razor	item

Write the spelling words with these first syllable spelling patterns.

Vowel sound in the first syllable

long   **short**

1. _____   9. _____

2. _____   10. _____

3. _____   11. _____

4. _____   12. _____

5. _____   13. _____

6. _____   14. _____

7. _____   15. _____

8. _____   16. _____

                                                      17. _____

                                                      18. _____

                                                      19. _____

                                                      20. _____

20

Grade 4/Unit 2
**Justin and the Best Biscuits
in the World**

35

Syllable Patterns

biscuit	bandage	mitten	pupil	fancy
clover	cabin	knapsack	sofa	limit
public	plastic	local	welcome	famous
oven	radar	mustard	razor	item

What's the Connection?

Complete each statement with a spelling word.

1. Clothing is to jacket as shelter is to _____.

2. Cap is to beret as glove is to _____.

3. Box is to carton as duffel bag is to _____.

4. Jam is to toast as butter is to _____.

5. Animal is to horse as plant is to _____.

6. Cotton is to nylon as wood is to _____.

7. Shut is to open as private is to _____.

8. Up is to down as plain is to _____.

9. Educate is to teacher as learn is to _____.

10. Dig is to shovel as shave is to _____.

11. Tiny is to huge as unknown is to _____.

12. Far is to near as widespread is to _____.

13. Fruit is to apple as furniture is to _____.

14. Salt is to pepper as ketchup is to _____.

15. Leave is to good-bye as enter is to _____.

Syllable Patterns

Proofreading Activity

There are six spelling mistakes in the letter below. Circle the misspelled words. Write the words correctly on the lines below.

Dear Justin,

     Thanks so much for the postcard! I wish I could live in a cabun and ride the range with you and your grandpa. I'd also like to taste some of his stewed raisins and pork, but most of all I'd like a biscut. Yummy! I didn't know you could bake without an ovin. By the way, I have a book about Nate Love and some other famus cowboys. They sure did some fancie circle roping and riding. There was no limut to their talents. You can borrow the book when you get home. See you soon.

                                Your friend,
                                Jamie

1. _____   3. _____   5. _____

2. _____   4. _____   6. _____

Writing Activity

Suppose you are Justin's friend. Write him a letter describing what you've been doing while he's been away. Use at least four spelling words in your letter.

_____

_____

_____

_____

Syllable Patterns

Look at the words in each set below. One word in each set is spelled correctly. Use a pencil to fill in the circle next to the correct word. Before you begin, look at the sample sets of words. Sample A has been done for you. Do Sample B by yourself. When you are sure you know what to do, you may go on with the rest of the page.

Sample A
- Ⓐ lemin
- Ⓑ lemmon
- Ⓒ lemon
- Ⓓ lemun

Sample B
- Ⓔ razin
- Ⓕ raison
- Ⓖ raizin
- Ⓗ raisin

1.
- Ⓐ limmit
- Ⓑ limit
- Ⓒ limut
- Ⓓ limitt

6.
- Ⓔ publick
- Ⓕ pubblic
- Ⓖ public
- Ⓗ publik

11.
- Ⓐ fansy
- Ⓑ fanncy
- Ⓒ fancy
- Ⓓ fancie

16.
- Ⓔ pupil
- Ⓕ puppil
- Ⓖ pupill
- Ⓗ puepil

2.
- Ⓔ welcome
- Ⓕ wellcome
- Ⓖ welcum
- Ⓗ welkcome

7.
- Ⓐ item
- Ⓑ itim
- Ⓒ itum
- Ⓓ ittem

12.
- Ⓔ musterd
- Ⓕ mustard
- Ⓖ mustrad
- Ⓗ musturd

17.
- Ⓐ ofven
- Ⓑ ovin
- Ⓒ ovun
- Ⓓ oven

3.
- Ⓐ napsac
- Ⓑ knapsac
- Ⓒ knapsak
- Ⓓ knapsack

8.
- Ⓔ rayzor
- Ⓕ razer
- Ⓖ raisor
- Ⓗ razor

13.
- Ⓐ mitten
- Ⓑ miten
- Ⓒ mittin
- Ⓓ mittun

18.
- Ⓔ clofer
- Ⓕ clover
- Ⓖ cloaver
- Ⓗ clowver

4.
- Ⓔ plastick
- Ⓕ plastik
- Ⓖ plastic
- Ⓗ plasic

9.
- Ⓐ sofa
- Ⓑ soffa
- Ⓒ soafa
- Ⓓ sowfa

14.
- Ⓔ faymous
- Ⓕ famus
- Ⓖ famis
- Ⓗ famous

19.
- Ⓐ biskuit
- Ⓑ biscut
- Ⓒ biscuit
- Ⓓ biskit

5.
- Ⓐ bandage
- Ⓑ bandadge
- Ⓒ bandidge
- Ⓓ bandudge

10.
- Ⓔ raydar
- Ⓕ radar
- Ⓖ raddar
- Ⓗ raidar

15.
- Ⓐ cabbin
- Ⓑ cabun
- Ⓒ cabin
- Ⓓ caben

20.
- Ⓔ lowcal
- Ⓕ loccal
- Ⓖ locul
- Ⓗ local

Words with Consonant Clusters

Pretest Directions

Fold back the paper along the dotted line. Use the blanks to write each word as it is read aloud. When you finish the test, unfold the paper. Use the list at the right to correct any spelling mistakes. Practice the words that you missed for the Posttest.

To Parents

Here are the results of your child's weekly spelling Pretest. You can help your child study for the Posttest by following these simple steps for each word on the word list:

1. Read the word to your child.

2. Have your child write the word, saying each letter as it is written.

3. Say each letter of the word as your child checks the spelling.

4. If a mistake has been made, have your child read each letter of the correctly spelled word aloud, then repeat steps 1–3.

1. _____
2. _____
3. _____
4. _____
5. _____
6. _____
7. _____
8. _____
9. _____
10. _____
11. _____
12. _____
13. _____
14. _____
15. _____
16. _____
17. _____
18. _____
19. _____
20. _____

1. blank
2. daring
3. claim
4. flour
5. crack
6. bridge
7. float
8. plank
9. classified
10. cradle
11. brand
12. among
13. flatter
14. clothesline
15. bridle
16. credit
17. darling
18. flutter
19. clatter
20. cruise

Challenge Words

_____
_____
_____
_____
_____

bulging
crumpled
haze
shrieking
waddled

Words with Consonant Clusters

Using the Word Study Steps

1. LOOK at the word.

2. SAY the word aloud.

3. STUDY the letters in the word.

4. WRITE the word.

5. CHECK the word.

   Did you spell the word right?
   If not, go back to step 1.

Spelling Tip

Use words you know how to spell to help you spell new words.

<u>br</u>avery + ju<u>dge</u> = <u>br</u>i<u>dge</u>

Word Scramble

Unscramble each set of letters to make a spelling word.

1. ourfl _____

2. miacl _____

3. ackcr _____

4. ridbeg _____

5. ankbl _____

6. grinda _____

7. toalf _____

8. fidelassic _____

9. darcle _____

10. dranb _____

11. knalp _____

12. gonma _____

13. taterlf _____

14. thesenilloc _____

15. dicert _____

16. dribel _____

17. gnarldi _____

18. rettulf _____

19. latertc _____

20. resuic _____

To Parents or Helpers

Using the Word Study Steps above as your child comes across any new words will help him or her learn to spell words effectively. Review the steps as you both go over this week's spelling words.

Go over the Spelling Tip with your child. Help your child use words he or she knows to figure out how to spell new words on the spelling list.

Help your child complete the spelling activity.

Words with Consonant Clusters

blank	crack	classified	flatter	darling
daring	bridge	cradle	clothesline	flutter
claim	float	brand	bridle	clatter
flour	plank	among	credit	cruise

Write the spelling words with these spelling patterns

words beginning with *fl*

1. _____
2. _____
3. _____
4. _____

words beginning with *cl*

5. _____
6. _____
7. _____
8. _____

words beginning with *cr*

9. _____
10. _____
11. _____
12. _____

words beginning with *br*

13. _____
14. _____
15. _____

words ending with *ng*

16. _____
17. _____
18. _____

words ending with *nk*

19. _____
20. _____

Sounds Alike

Write the spelling word that rhymes with each word below.

21. name _____
22. sharing _____
23. track _____

24. butter _____
25. lose _____

Name_____ Date_____

Words with Consonant Clusters

blank	crack	classified	flatter	darling
daring	bridge	cradle	clothesline	flutter
claim	float	brand	bridle	clatter
flour	plank	among	credit	cruise

Complete each sentence below with a spelling word.

1. When it's windy, the leaves _____ and shake.

2. The children helped to hang the laundry on the _____.

3. We mixed milk and _____ to make biscuits.

4. The horse rider removed the saddle and _____.

5. The carpenter replaced a wooden _____ that had rotted.

6. It took great _____ to dive into the stormy sea.

7. We read an ad in the _____ section.

8. Ranchers _____ their cattle to show who owns them.

9. Did anyone _____ the ring you found in the parking lot?

10. Our teacher will give us extra _____ if we read a book.

Word Meaning: Synonyms
Write the spelling word that has the same or almost the same meaning.

11. sweety _____   15. voyage _____

12. amid _____   16. break _____

13. overpass _____   17. empty _____

14. baby bed _____   18. crash _____

Challenge Extension: Write one fill-in sentence for
each Challenge Word and then exchange papers with a
partner to complete them.

42

Grade 4/Unit 2
Just a Dream 18

Words with Consonant Clusters

Proofreading Activity

There are six spelling mistakes in Walter's journal entry below. Circle the misspelled words. Write the words correctly on the lines below.

October 28

What a shocking dream I had! I saw the world in the future. Garbage was piled so high I had to use a brigde to get from one side of town to the other. The air was so dirty that the laundry on a closeline actually turned black. I got caught amung thousands of cars in a gigantic traffic jam, with thousands of horns honking. The clattur was so unbearable that I covered my ears to block the noise. The rivers and lakes were so polluted that a person would have to be very dairing —or crazy—to go swimming. I was glad when I finally woke up in my room. I hope that the future world will not be like this, as some people clame it may be.

1. _____   3. _____   5. _____

2. _____   4. _____   6. _____

Writing Activity

Have you ever had a dream about the future? Write about one of your dreams. Use four spelling words in your writing.

_____

_____

_____

_____

Words with Consonant Clusters

Look at the words in each set below. One word in each set is spelled correctly. Use a pencil to fill in the circle next to the correct word. Before you begin, look at the sample sets of words. Sample A has been done for you. Do Sample B by yourself. When you are sure you know what to do, you may go on with the rest of the page.

Sample A
Ⓐ clothez
Ⓑ clothes
Ⓒ klothes
Ⓓ clowes

Sample B
Ⓐ bireak
Ⓑ brek
Ⓒ break
Ⓓ breack

1.
Ⓐ blank
Ⓑ blangk
Ⓒ blanck
Ⓓ blanc

6.
Ⓔ fluttur
Ⓕ flutter
Ⓖ fluttir
Ⓗ fluttor

11.
Ⓐ bridge
Ⓑ brige
Ⓒ brigde
Ⓓ bidge

16.
Ⓔ amung
Ⓕ ammong
Ⓖ amonk
Ⓗ among

2.
Ⓔ cruse
Ⓕ kruse
Ⓖ cruize
Ⓗ cruise

7.
Ⓐ flowr
Ⓑ flourr
Ⓒ flour
Ⓓ fluor

12.
Ⓔ clothsline
Ⓕ closeline
Ⓖ clozeline
Ⓗ clothesline

17.
Ⓐ classified
Ⓑ classifide
Ⓒ clasiffied
Ⓓ classfied

3.
Ⓐ dareing
Ⓑ daring
Ⓒ dairing
Ⓓ darink

8.
Ⓔ credit
Ⓕ creddit
Ⓖ kredit
Ⓗ creditt

13.
Ⓐ flote
Ⓑ flowt
Ⓒ float
Ⓓ floet

18.
Ⓔ brande
Ⓕ branned
Ⓖ brannd
Ⓗ brand

4.
Ⓔ clattur
Ⓕ clattir
Ⓖ clatter
Ⓗ cladder

9.
Ⓐ krak
Ⓑ crac
Ⓒ crak
Ⓓ crack

14.
Ⓔ flater
Ⓕ flatter
Ⓖ flattur
Ⓗ flattir

19.
Ⓐ darrling
Ⓑ darling
Ⓒ darlingk
Ⓓ darlink

5.
Ⓐ clame
Ⓑ claim
Ⓒ klame
Ⓓ klaim

10.
Ⓔ bridel
Ⓕ bridle
Ⓖ briddle
Ⓗ briddel

15.
Ⓐ planck
Ⓑ plank
Ⓒ plang
Ⓓ plangk

20.
Ⓔ cradel
Ⓕ craddle
Ⓖ craydel
Ⓗ cradle

Words with Consonant Clusters

Pretest Directions

Fold back the paper along the dotted line. Use the blanks to write each word as it is read aloud. When you finish the test, unfold the paper. Use the list at the right to correct any spelling mistakes. Practice the words you missed for the Posttest.

To Parents

Here are the results of your child's weekly spelling Pretest. You can help your child study for the Posttest by following these simple steps for each word on the word list:

1. Read the word to your child.

2. Have your child write the word, saying each letter as it is written.

3. Say each letter of the word as your child checks the spelling.

4. If a mistake has been made, have your child read each letter of the correctly spelled word aloud, then repeat steps 1–3.

1. _____	1. thrill
2. _____	2. spruce
3. _____	3. stand
4. _____	4. speed
5. _____	5. stretch
6. _____	6. sprint
7. _____	7. spare
8. _____	8. threw
9. _____	9. stranger
10. _____	10. springtime
11. _____	11. stern
12. _____	12. spectacle
13. _____	13. strap
14. _____	14. thrifty
15. _____	15. street
16. _____	16. stung
17. _____	17. sparkle
18. _____	18. stress
19. _____	19. special
20. _____	20. steak

Challenge Words

_____ clustered

_____ county

_____ glistened

_____ overflowing

_____ sturdy

Name_____ Date_____

Words with Consonant Clusters

Using the Word Study Steps

1. LOOK at the word.

2. SAY the word aloud.

3. STUDY the letters in the word.

4. WRITE the word.

5. CHECK the word.

    Did you spell the word right?
    If not, go back to step 1.

Find and Circle

Find and circle the hidden spelling words.

```
a z t h r i l l z x x s p r u c e a w s t a n d b n u s p e e d a a

s t r e t c h x x s p r i n t x a s p a r e z z z t h r e w b w x x v

s t r a n g e r a a b s p r i n g t i m e w a l m e w x s t e r n x

z s p e c t a c l e x x v s t r a p z z x t h r i f t y a a b s t r e e t

x x x s t u n g k k x x v x x x s p a r k l e x x v s t r e s s x x

z s p e c i a l x a b h n i s n x x s t e a k a a v x x x v v v s
```

To Parents or Helpers

    Using the Word Study Steps above as your child comes across any new words will help him or her learn to spell words effectively. Review the steps as you both go over this week's spelling words.
    Go over the Spelling Tip with your child. Ask your child if he or she knows other clues to help remember spelling words. Help him or her use the clues and then write the spelling words to remember how to spell them.
    Help your child find and circle the hidden spelling words.

Words with Consonant Clusters

thrill	stretch	stranger	strap	sparkle
spruce	sprint	springtime	thrifty	stress
stand	spare	stern	street	special
speed	threw	spectacle	stung	steak

Pattern Power
Write the spelling words with these spelling patterns.

words beginning with *str*

1. _____
2. _____
3. _____
4. _____
5. _____

words beginning with *sp*

6. _____
7. _____
8. _____
9. _____
10. _____

words beginning with *st*

11. _____
12. _____
13. _____
14. _____

words beginning with *spr*

15. _____
16. _____
17. _____

words beginning with *thr*

18. _____
19. _____
20. _____

Rhyme Time
Write the spelling word that rhymes with each word.

21. goose _____   24. among _____

22. lead _____   25. learn _____

23. shoe _____

Words with Consonant Clusters

thrill	stretch	stranger	strap	sparkle
spruce	sprint	springtime	thrifty	stress
stand	spare	stern	street	special
speed	threw	spectacle	stung	steak

Finish the Word
Write the missing letters to correctly complete the words in the sentences.

"Hurry up," my parents called. "There's not a minute to **1.** sp_____.
We don't want to be late. We'll wait for you in the car."

I grabbed my cap, tightened the **2.** str_____ on my fanny pack, and
ran out the door to the car.

Every April, our city holds a **3.** spr_____ festival, beginning with a
parade. It is always a very **4.** sp_____ event. This year's parade was an
eye-popping **5.** sp_____. It was a **6.** thr_____ for children and
adults alike. Dozens of bands and floats made their way down the one-mile **7.**
str_____ of Fifth Avenue, the main **8.** str_____ in our city. My
brother and I like to **9.** st_____ along the curb near City Hall. That's
where the parade will slow down for the mayor and then **10.** sp_____ up
again. This year our sister is in the high school marching band. We watched as
she and the other twirlers **11.** thr_____ their batons up in the air and then
caught them. The sunlight hit the beads and sequins on their outfits and made
them **12.** sp_____. What a sight! We cheered loudly as they marched
past us.

Word Groups
Write the spelling word that belongs in each group.

13. pierced, pricked, _____

14. fir, pine, _____

15. strain, pressure, _____

16. economical, penny-wise, _____

17. race, run, _____

18. alien, foreigner, _____

19. harsh, strict, _____

20. chop, burger, _____

48   **Challenge Extension:**
Write a sentence for each Challenge Word.

Grade 4/Unit 2
Leah's Pony | 20 |

Words with Consonant Clusters

Proofreading Activity

There are six spelling mistakes in this short story. Circle the misspelled words. Write the words correctly on the lines below.

Leah was my best friend. I got a letter from her last month. She told me about the speshal way she saved her family's farm. I wish I could have seen the expression on the auctioneer's face when Leah offered him one dollar for her father's tractor!

We lost our farm in the sprinktime, and then we moved to Oregon. I haven't seen Leah in a year. Whenever I have a few spair pennies for a stamp, I write to her.

Life has been difficult for farm families everywhere because of the drought. We had to be as thirfty as we could. We thruw nothing away, not even empty flour sacks. My mama used the material to make clothes for my sister and me. She could even make a pot of soup strech for three or four meals. Times were difficult, but they will get better.

1. _____ 3. _____ 5. _____

2. _____ 4. _____ 6. _____

Writing Activity

What do you think Leah said in her letter? Pretend you are Leah. Write a letter telling about the auction. Use four spelling words in your writing.

_____

_____

_____

_____

Words with Consonant Clusters

Look at the words in each set below. One word in each set is spelled correctly. Use a pencil to fill in the circle next to the correct word. Before you begin, look at the sample sets of words. Sample A has been done for you. Do Sample B by yourself. When you are sure you know what to do, you may go on with the rest of the page.

Sample A
- Ⓐ springkle
- Ⓑ sprinkel
- Ⓒ springle
- ⬤ sprinkle

Sample B
- Ⓐ threaten
- Ⓑ threatin
- Ⓒ threten
- Ⓓ threaton

1.
- Ⓐ sturn
- Ⓑ stren
- Ⓒ stern
- Ⓓ sternn

6.
- Ⓔ strapp
- Ⓕ strape
- Ⓖ starp
- Ⓗ strap

11.
- Ⓐ strech
- Ⓑ stertch
- Ⓒ stretch
- Ⓓ sturetch

16.
- Ⓔ thrill
- Ⓕ thirll
- Ⓖ thruill
- Ⓗ thril

2.
- Ⓔ spingtime
- Ⓕ springtime
- Ⓖ sprinktime
- Ⓗ sprngtime

7.
- Ⓐ spare
- Ⓑ spair
- Ⓒ spayr
- Ⓓ spaire

12.
- Ⓔ spead
- Ⓕ speed
- Ⓖ spede
- Ⓗ speide

17.
- Ⓐ stak
- Ⓑ staik
- Ⓒ steak
- Ⓓ stacke

3.
- Ⓐ stranger
- Ⓑ strangure
- Ⓒ stanger
- Ⓓ strangur

8.
- Ⓔ thirfty
- Ⓕ thrifty
- Ⓖ thrfty
- Ⓗ thifty

13.
- Ⓐ stung
- Ⓑ stong
- Ⓒ stug
- Ⓓ stunge

18.
- Ⓔ sparkle
- Ⓕ spearkle
- Ⓖ sparckle
- Ⓗ sprakle

4.
- Ⓔ specktakle
- Ⓕ spektacle
- Ⓖ specticle
- Ⓗ spectacle

9.
- Ⓐ sprint
- Ⓑ spirnt
- Ⓒ sprnt
- Ⓓ spint

14.
- Ⓔ stande
- Ⓕ stend
- Ⓖ stanned
- Ⓗ stand

19.
- Ⓐ streass
- Ⓑ stress
- Ⓒ sterss
- Ⓓ stres

5.
- Ⓐ thrugh
- Ⓑ threw
- Ⓒ thriew
- Ⓓ thruw

10.
- Ⓔ streat
- Ⓕ streit
- Ⓖ stareet
- Ⓗ street

15.
- Ⓐ spurce
- Ⓑ spruse
- Ⓒ spruce
- Ⓓ sproose

20.
- Ⓔ specail
- Ⓕ spacial
- Ⓖ speshal
- Ⓗ special

Plurals

Pretest Directions

Fold back the paper along the dotted line. Use the blanks to write each word as it is read aloud. When you finish the test, unfold the paper. Use the list at the right to correct any spelling mistakes. Practice the words you missed for the Posttest.

To Parents

Here are the results of your child's weekly spelling Pretest. You can help your child study for the Posttest by following these simple steps for each word on the word list:

1. Read the word to your child.

2. Have your child write the word, saying each letter as it is written.

3. Say each letter of the word as your child checks the spelling.

4. If a mistake has been made, have your child read each letter of the correctly spelled word aloud, then repeat steps 1–3.

#	Answer	#	Word
1.	_____	1.	cities
2.	_____	2.	mistakes
3.	_____	3.	foxes
4.	_____	4.	babies
5.	_____	5.	knives
6.	_____	6.	engines
7.	_____	7.	soldiers
8.	_____	8.	ranches
9.	_____	9.	hobbies
10.	_____	10.	yourselves
11.	_____	11.	eyelashes
12.	_____	12.	uniforms
13.	_____	13.	batteries
14.	_____	14.	calves
15.	_____	15.	shovels
16.	_____	16.	sunglasses
17.	_____	17.	groceries
18.	_____	18.	loaves
19.	_____	19.	mattresses
20.	_____	20.	ferries

Challenge Words

_____ crate

_____ ditches

_____ endless

_____ glinting

_____ inning

Name_____ Date_____

Plurals

Using the Word Study Steps

1. LOOK at the word.

2. SAY the word aloud.

3. STUDY the letters in the word.

4. WRITE the word.

5. CHECK the word.

   Did you spell the word right?
   If not, go back to step 1.

Spelling Tip

Add -s to most words to form plurals.

string + s = strings

Add -es to words ending in x, z, s, sh, or ch.

stretch + es = stretches

When a word ends with a consonant followed by y, change the y to i and add -es.

memory + es = memories

To make plurals of words that end with one f or fe, you often need to change the f or fe to v and add -es.

Find Rhyming Words

Circle the word in each row that rhymes with the spelling word on the left.

1. **mistakes**	shakes	taken
2. **foxes**	books	boxes
3. **knives**	stoves	wives
4. **ranches**	thanks	branches
5. **hobbies**	cobbles	lobbies

6. **eyelashes**	flashes	laughs
7. **calves**	curves	halves
8. **sunglasses**	grass	masses
9. **loaves**	stoves	coats
10. **ferries**	berries	furry

To Parents or Helpers

Using the Word Study Steps above as your child comes across any new words will help him or her learn to spell words effectively. Review the steps as you both go over this week's spelling words.

Go over each Spelling Tip with your child. Ask him or her to add -s or -es to form plurals. Ask if he or she knows other words that end with a consonant followed by y. Help your child to use the Spelling Tips to add endings to the words to make them plural.

Help your child find and circle the word in each row that doesn't rhyme with the spelling word.

Name_____ Date_____

Plurals

cities	knives	hobbies	batteries	groceries
mistakes	engines	yourselves	calves	loaves
foxes	soldiers	eyelashes	shovels	mattresses
babies	ranches	uniforms	sunglasses	ferries

Pattern Power

Write the spelling words that fit each of these plural endings.

-s

1. _____
2. _____
3. _____
4. _____
5. _____

-es

6. _____
7. _____
8. _____
9. _____
10. _____

-ies

11. _____
12. _____
13. _____
14. _____
15. _____
16. _____

-ves

17. _____
18. _____
19. _____
20. _____

All in Order

Write the following words in alphabetical order: *foxes, cities, babies, ferries, calves, knives, batteries, eyelashes, groceries, hobbies.*

1. _____
2. _____
3. _____
4. _____
5. _____

6. _____
7. _____
8. _____
9. _____
10. _____

Plurals

cities	knives	hobbies	batteries	groceries
mistakes	engines	yourselves	calves	loaves
foxes	soldiers	eyelashes	shovels	mattresses
babies	ranches	uniforms	sunglasses	ferries

What's the Word?

Write the spelling words that match the clues below.

1. where some live _____

2. cans of soup _____

3. kinds of ships _____

4. newborns _____

5. tools for snow _____

6. work clothes _____

7. on beds _____

8. all of you _____

9. make trains go _____

10. cut things _____

11. on eyelids _____

12. pastimes _____

What's the Word?

Complete each sentence below with a spelling word.

13. I made very few _____ on my math test.

14. The wild _____ had big, red, bushy tails.

15. The _____ were trained to fight battles.

16. There are many cattle _____ out West.

17. I got new _____ for my flashlight.

18. The farmer's cows had newborn _____ this year.

19. The sun was so bright, I put on my _____.

20. He went to the store to buy five _____ of bread.

Challenge Extension: Scramble the letters of each Challenge Word and write the scrambled words down. Exchange papers with a partner and unscramble each word.

Plurals

Writing Activity

There are six spelling mistakes in this paragraph. Circle the misspelled words. Write the words correctly on the lines below.

   During World War II, my family and many hundreds of other Japanese-American families from cityes and towns everywhere were forced to live in government camps. We were guarded by soldjers. It was a difficult time for all of us. It helped to pass the time by playing baseball. First we had to make a baseball field. We used shovles to clear away plants to make a space for the field. Then we packed down the dust and made it hard. Some men found wood for bleachers. Our mothers used the covers from mattressies to make uniformes for us. Our friends back home sent us bats, balls, and gloves. I was really nervous during the first game. I wasn't a very good player and didn't want to make any misteaks. Guess what? I hit a home run!

1. _____ 3. _____ 5. _____

2. _____ 4. _____ 6. _____

Writing Activity

If you could interview some of the people who once lived in the government camps, what questions would you ask them? Use four spelling words in your interview questions.

_____

_____

_____

_____

Plurals

Look at the words in each set below. One word in each set is spelled correctly. Use a pencil to fill in the circle next to the correct word. Before you begin, look at the sample sets of words. Sample A has been done for you. Do Sample B by yourself. When you are sure you know what to do, you may go on with the rest of the page.

Sample A
Ⓐ ladees
Ⓑ ladys
Ⓒ ladies
Ⓓ ladees

Sample B
Ⓐ berryes
Ⓑ berries
Ⓒ berrys
Ⓓ berriez

1. Ⓐ ferreez
   Ⓑ ferrys
   Ⓒ ferriez
   Ⓓ ferries

6. Ⓔ yorselves
   Ⓕ yourselves
   Ⓖ yourselvz
   Ⓗ yuorselves

11. Ⓐ cityes
    Ⓑ citees
    Ⓒ cities
    Ⓓ citys

16. Ⓔ eyelashs
    Ⓕ eyelashies
    Ⓖ eyelashes
    Ⓗ eyelatches

2. Ⓔ loaves
   Ⓕ loafes
   Ⓖ loavz
   Ⓗ loavez

7. Ⓐ ranchs
   Ⓑ ranchis
   Ⓒ ranches
   Ⓓ ranchez

12. Ⓔ foxez
    Ⓕ foxs
    Ⓖ foxies
    Ⓗ foxes

17. Ⓐ batterys
    Ⓑ battereez
    Ⓒ batteryes
    Ⓓ batteries

3. Ⓐ songlasses
   Ⓑ sunglasess
   Ⓒ sunglassez
   Ⓓ sunglasses

8. Ⓔ engines
   Ⓕ enginez
   Ⓖ engins
   Ⓗ enginz

13. Ⓐ knives
    Ⓑ knivez
    Ⓒ knivies
    Ⓓ knifez

18. Ⓔ shovles
    Ⓕ shovlez
    Ⓖ shovels
    Ⓗ shovals

4. Ⓔ calvs
   Ⓕ calvez
   Ⓖ calves
   Ⓗ claves

9. Ⓐ babees
   Ⓑ babys
   Ⓒ babiez
   Ⓓ babies

14. Ⓔ solders
    Ⓕ soljures
    Ⓖ soldierz
    Ⓗ soldiers

19. Ⓐ grossries
    Ⓑ groceryes
    Ⓒ grocerees
    Ⓓ groceries

5. Ⓐ yuniforms
   Ⓑ uniforms
   Ⓒ unifroms
   Ⓓ uniformz

10. Ⓔ misteaks
    Ⓕ mistakes
    Ⓖ mistaks
    Ⓗ misstakes

15. Ⓐ hobbies
    Ⓑ hobbyies
    Ⓒ hobbese
    Ⓓ hobbys

20. Ⓔ mattrusses
    Ⓕ mattreses
    Ⓖ mattresses
    Ⓗ mattrasses

Name_____ Date_____

Words from Social Studies

Pretest Directions

Fold back the paper along the dotted line. Use the blanks to write each word as it is read aloud. When you finish the test, unfold the paper. Use the list at the right to correct any spelling mistakes. Practice the words you missed for the Posttest.

To Parents

Here are the results of your child's weekly spelling Pretest. You can help your child study for the Posttest by following these simple steps for each word on the word list:

1. Read the word to your child.

2. Have your child write the word, saying each letter as it is written.

3. Say each letter of the word as your child checks the spelling.

4. If a mistake has been made, have your child read each letter of the correctly spelled word aloud, then repeat steps 1–3.

1. _____	1. language
2. _____	2. history
3. _____	3. pottery
4. _____	4. study
5. _____	5. spoken
6. _____	6. accent
7. _____	7. tribe
8. _____	8. human
9. _____	9. custom
10. _____	10. village
11. _____	11. folktale
12. _____	12. practice
13. _____	13. relatives
14. _____	14. interview
15. _____	15. region
16. _____	16. symbol
17. _____	17. guide
18. _____	18. totem
19. _____	19. colony
20. _____	20. prints

Challenge Words

_____ extinct

_____ native

_____ backgrounds

_____ generations

_____ century

Name_____ Date_____

Words from Social Studies

Using the Word Study Steps

1. LOOK at the word.

2. SAY the word aloud.

3. STUDY the letters in the word.

4. WRITE the word.

5. CHECK the word.

   Did you spell the word right?
   If not, go back to step 1.

Spelling Tip

Become familiar with the dictionary and use it often.

Word Scramble

Unscramble each set of letters to make a spelling word.

1. skepon _____

2. idgue _____

3. muhna _____

4. coolyn _____

5. anglegau _____

6. tolkleaf _____

7. latesiver _____

8. blosmy _____

9. metto _____

10. carpicet _____

11. rhytiso _____

12. vieinwert _____

13. biter _____

14. legliva _____

15. strinp _____

16. dyust _____

17. engior _____

18. mustoc _____

19. rotpety _____

20. necact _____

To Parents or Helpers

    Using the Word Study Steps above as your child comes across any new words will help him or her learn to spell words effectively. Review the steps as you both go over this week's spelling words.

    Go over the Spelling Tip with your child. Help him or her look up the spelling words in the dictionary.

    Help your child unscramble the spelling words.

Words from Social Studies

language	spoken	custom	relatives	guide
history	accent	village	interview	totem
pottery	tribe	folktale	region	colony
study	human	practice	symbol	prints

Vowel Power

Write the spelling words that fit each of these vowel sounds:

**short a in the
first syllable**

**short i in the
first syllable**

1. _____   4. _____   7. _____
2. _____   5. _____   8. _____
3. _____   6. _____

**short u in the
first syllable**

**short o in the
first syllable**

**short e in the
first syllable**

9. _____   11. _____   13. _____
10. _____   12. _____

**long o in the
first syllable**

**long i in the
first syllable**

**long u in the
first syllable**

14. _____   17. _____   19. _____
15. _____   18. _____
16. _____

**long e in the
first syllable**

20. _____

Words from Social Studies

language	spoken	custom	relatives	guide
history	accent	village	interview	totem
pottery	tribe	folktale	region	colony
study	human	practice	symbol	prints

Complete each sentence below with a spelling word.

1. Spanish is _____ here.

2. I live in a mountainous _____.

3. We met the artist who made this _____.

4. What _____ did Geronimo belong to?

5. Dad will go to an _____ for a new job.

6. I plan to _____ music in college.

7. What _____ do you speak?

8. The _____ led us along the trail.

9. We read your _____ of what happened.

10. _____ beings come in all shapes and sizes.

11. I _____ piano for one hour each day.

12. Where do your _____ live?

13. I just read a funny _____ from Russia.

14. The lion is a _____ of courage.

15. The artist carved and painted a _____ pole.

16. It is a _____ in my family to drink tea before lunch.

Challenge Extension: Have students write a fill in the blank for each Challenge Word, then exchange papers with a partner and complete each other's sentences.

Words from Social Studies

Proofreading Activity

There are six spelling mistakes in this paragraph. Circle the misspelled words.
Write the words correctly on the lines below.

Did you know that Choctaw is an endangered Native American langauge?
It is only spokin by 12,000 people, today. An organization working to keep alive
Choctaw and other Native American languages prins books and makes records
available for people to use. In histry class we are learning Choctaw words and
phrases. One of the girls is a member of the Choctaw trieb. She and her relitives
speak Choctaw at home. Some of us would like to study Choctaw. I know it will
take a lot of practice because it is so different from English.

1. _____   3. _____   5. _____

2. _____   4. _____   6. _____

Writing Activity

Imagine that the year is 1800 and that you are a Native American child. Write a
paragraph about what life is like among your people, using four spelling words.

_____

_____

_____

_____

Words from Social Studies

Look at the words in each set below. One word in each set is spelled correctly. Use a pencil to fill in the circle next to the correct word. Before you begin, look at the sample sets of words. Sample A has been done for you. Do Sample B by yourself. When you are sure you know what to do, you may go on with the rest of the page.

Sample A
- (A) science
- (B) sience
- (C) sciense
- (D) siense

Sample B
- (E) natuve
- (F) native
- (G) nativ
- (H) nattive

1.
- (A) prins
- (B) prints
- (C) printz
- (D) prinz

2.
- (E) language
- (F) langage
- (G) langwage
- (H) langauge

3.
- (A) colny
- (B) colonny
- (C) colony
- (D) coluny

4.
- (E) histry
- (F) histrey
- (G) historie
- (H) history

5.
- (A) totum
- (B) totim
- (C) totem
- (D) tottem

6.
- (E) pottery
- (F) potery
- (G) pottry
- (H) pottary

7.
- (A) guyde
- (B) guide
- (C) giude
- (D) gide

8.
- (E) studie
- (F) studdy
- (G) study
- (H) studie

9.
- (A) simble
- (B) symble
- (C) symbowl
- (D) symbol

10.
- (E) spokin
- (F) spoken
- (G) spocken
- (H) spockin

11.
- (A) region
- (B) regin
- (C) regun
- (D) regon

12.
- (E) acent
- (F) akcent
- (G) acsent
- (H) accent

13.
- (A) intreview
- (B) intrview
- (C) interview
- (D) innerview

14.
- (E) trieb
- (F) tribe
- (G) trybe
- (H) tirbe

15.
- (A) reltives
- (B) relitives
- (C) relutives
- (D) relatives

16.
- (E) humun
- (F) huemin
- (G) human
- (H) humeman

17.
- (A) practice
- (B) practise
- (C) practus
- (D) pracktise

18.
- (E) costum
- (F) custom
- (G) cusstom
- (H) custim

19.
- (A) foketail
- (B) folktale
- (C) fowktale
- (D) folktail

20.
- (E) villuge
- (F) villige
- (G) vilage
- (H) village

Grade 4/Unit 2 Review Test

Read each sentence. If an underlined word is spelled wrong, fill in the circle that goes with that word. If no word is spelled wrong, fill in the circle below NONE. Read Sample A, and do Sample B.

A. She took her <u>sunglasses</u> and a <u>napsack</u> to the <u>cabin</u>.
                 A   B   C

A. Ⓐ ⬤Ⓑ Ⓒ Ⓓ   NONE

B. We put the <u>sleepy</u> <u>babies</u> in the <u>cradle</u>.
              E   F   G

B. Ⓔ Ⓕ Ⓖ Ⓗ   NONE

1. The explosion <u>amonng</u> the <u>soldiers</u> made a <u>spectacle</u>.
                 A   B   C

1. Ⓐ Ⓑ Ⓒ Ⓓ   NONE

2. The <u>colony</u> had <u>clover</u> fields and <u>spruice</u> trees.
        E   F   G

2. Ⓔ Ⓕ Ⓖ Ⓗ   NONE

3. The <u>raizer</u> cut <u>stung</u> so I covered it with a <u>bandage</u>.
        A   B   C

3. Ⓐ Ⓑ Ⓒ Ⓓ   NONE

4. The <u>thrifty</u> man divided one <u>biscit</u> <u>among</u> his friends.
        E   F   G

4. Ⓔ Ⓕ Ⓖ Ⓗ   NONE

5. The men in the <u>colonee</u> used <u>shovels</u> to dig for <u>pottery</u>.
               A   B   C

5. Ⓐ Ⓑ Ⓒ Ⓓ   NONE

6. The <u>thrifty</u> owner repaired the <u>crack</u> in her <u>totim</u> pole.
        E   F   G

6. Ⓔ Ⓕ Ⓖ Ⓗ   NONE

7. When she is under <u>stress</u> her <u>eyelashs</u> <u>flutter</u>.
                     A   B   C

7. Ⓐ Ⓑ Ⓒ Ⓓ   NONE

8. This <u>foketale</u> describes a <u>bridle</u> and a <u>totem</u> pole.
       E   F   G

8. Ⓔ Ⓕ Ⓖ Ⓗ   NONE

9. A <u>bandage</u> will not hold the <u>plank</u> between the <u>ferrys</u>.
      A   B   C

9. Ⓐ Ⓑ Ⓒ Ⓓ   NONE

10. Our <u>calves</u> <u>stung</u> from all that <u>fancy</u> dancing.
        E   F   G

10. Ⓔ Ⓕ Ⓖ Ⓗ   NONE

11. We sat in the <u>clover</u> to hear a man with an <u>acent</u> tell a <u>folktale</u>.
              A   B   C

11. Ⓐ Ⓑ Ⓒ Ⓓ   NONE

Go on →

Grade 4 Unit 2 Review Test

12. The <u>ferries</u> carried <u>soldyiers</u> to the <u>colony</u>.
         E   F   G
12. Ⓔ Ⓕ Ⓖ NONE Ⓗ

13. The <u>stres</u> on the <u>plank</u> caused it to <u>crack</u>.
         A   B   C
13. Ⓐ Ⓑ Ⓒ NONE Ⓓ

14. We saw <u>calves</u> eating <u>clovir</u> stuck in a <u>bridle</u>.
             E   F   G
14. Ⓔ Ⓕ Ⓖ NONE Ⓗ

15. Watching them <u>fluter</u> <u>among</u> the flowers was a <u>spectacle</u>.
                  A   B   C
15. Ⓐ Ⓑ Ⓒ NONE Ⓓ

16. To be <u>fancy</u>, she will <u>spruce</u> up with fake <u>eyelashes</u>.
        E   F   G
16. Ⓔ Ⓕ Ⓖ NONE Ⓗ

17. The <u>stress</u> on the horse's <u>bridal</u> caused it to <u>crack</u>.
         A   B   C
17. Ⓐ Ⓑ Ⓒ NONE Ⓓ

18. She ate a <u>biscuit</u> and told a <u>folktale</u> in a French <u>accent</u>.
           E   F   G
18. Ⓔ Ⓕ Ⓖ NONE Ⓗ

19. We loaded the <u>ferries</u> with <u>potterie</u> and <u>shovels</u>.
             A   B   C
19. Ⓐ Ⓑ Ⓒ NONE Ⓓ

20. Don't use a <u>razor</u> to cut a <u>planck</u> from that <u>spruce</u>.
          E   F   G
20. Ⓔ Ⓕ Ⓖ NONE Ⓗ

21. It was a <u>spectacle</u> seeing the <u>calfs</u> share one <u>biscuit</u>.
            A   B   C
21. Ⓐ Ⓑ Ⓒ NONE Ⓓ

22. He saw her <u>eyelashes</u> <u>flutter</u> after she was <u>stunng</u>.
            E   F   G
22. Ⓔ Ⓕ Ⓖ NONE Ⓗ

23. A <u>bandage</u> is a <u>thriftie</u> way to hide that <u>fancy</u> ring.
        A   B   C
23. Ⓐ Ⓑ Ⓒ NONE Ⓓ

24. The boy with the <u>accent</u> engraves <u>pottery</u> with a <u>razor</u>.
                 E   F   G
24. Ⓔ Ⓕ Ⓖ NONE Ⓗ

25. The <u>soldiers</u> used <u>shovles</u> to dig out the <u>totem</u> pole.
         A   B   C
25. Ⓐ Ⓑ Ⓒ NONE Ⓓ

Words with /ou/ and /oi/

Pretest Directions

Fold back the paper along the dotted line. Use the blanks to write each word as it is read aloud. When you finish the test, unfold the paper. Use the list at the right to correct any spelling mistakes. Practice the words you missed for the Posttest.

To Parents

Here are the results of your child's weekly spelling Pretest. You can help your child study for the Posttest by following these simple steps for each word on the word list:

1. Read the word to your child.

2. Have your child write the word, saying each letter as it is written.

3. Say each letter of the word as your child checks the spelling.

4. If a mistake has been made, have your child read each letter of the correctly spelled word aloud, and then repeat steps 1–3.

#		#	
1.	_____	1.	oily
2.	_____	2.	annoy
3.	_____	3.	around
4.	_____	4.	growl
5.	_____	5.	disappoint
6.	_____	6.	royalty
7.	_____	7.	bounce
8.	_____	8.	bowing
9.	_____	9.	moist
10.	_____	10.	enjoyment
11.	_____	11.	aloud
12.	_____	12.	tower
13.	_____	13.	avoid
14.	_____	14.	employ
15.	_____	15.	lookout
16.	_____	16.	however
17.	_____	17.	appointment
18.	_____	18.	scout
19.	_____	19.	powder
20.	_____	20.	noun

Challenge Words

_____   admitted

_____   displaying

_____   elegantly

_____   strolling

_____   wharf

Words with /ou/ and /oi/

Using the Word Study Steps

1. LOOK at the word.

2. SAY the word aloud.

3. STUDY the letters in the word.

4. WRITE the word.

5. CHECK the word.

   Did you spell the word right?
   If not, go back to step 1.

Spelling Tips

Think of a word you know that has the same spelling pattern as the word you want to spell.

sc<u>ou</u>t b<u>ou</u>nce ar<u>ou</u>nd

Word Scramble

Unscramble each set of letters to make a spelling word.

1. loiy	_____	**11.** tylyora	_____
2. idvoa	_____	**12.** tsmoi	_____
3. kuoootl	_____	**13.** ntiopapntem	_____
4. olmepy	_____	**14.** necuob	_____
5. verwohe	_____	**15.** wniogb	_____
6. tousc	_____	**16.** uonn	_____
7. drewop	_____	**17.** rlwog	_____
8. ppnotiasid	_____	**18.** mtneyojen	_____
9. yonan	_____	**19.** ludoa	_____
10. nuodra	_____	**20.** woter	_____

To Parents or Helpers

Using the Word Study Steps above as your child comes across any new words will help him or her learn to spell words effectively. Review the steps as you both go over this week's spelling words.

Go over each Spelling Tip with your child. Help your child look at some of the spelling words to see which ones have the same spelling pattern.

Help your child complete the word scramble.

Words with /ou/ and /oi/

oily	disappoint	moist	avoid	appointment
annoy	royalty	enjoyment	employ	scout
around	bounce	aloud	lookout	powder
growl	bowing	tower	however	noun

Pattern Power!

Write the spelling words with these spelling patterns.

oi

1. _____
2. _____
3. _____
4. _____
5. _____

oy

6. _____
7. _____
8. _____
9. _____

ou

10. _____
11. _____
12. _____
13. _____
14. _____
15. _____

ow

16. _____
17. _____
18. _____
19. _____
20. _____

Words with /ou/ and /oi/

oily	disappoint	moist	avoid	appointment
annoy	royalty	enjoyment	employ	scout
around	bounce	aloud	lookout	powder
growl	bowing	tower	however	noun

What's the Word?

Complete each sentence with a word from the spelling list.

1. The baby likes to look _____ to see what is going on.

2. Keep the soil around the plant _____ or the plant will die.

3. Did you make an _____ to see the dentist?

4. A king and a queen are _____.

5. What a loud _____ that dog made!

6. The wet road had a slick, _____ coating from all of the traffic.

7. I really like that dress; _____, I can't buy it now.

8. Do you like to read stories _____ to younger children?

9. In the old days, _____ was a polite form of greeting.

10. Mom gets a lot of _____ out of working in the garden.

What Do You Mean?

Read each dictionary definition below. Then write the spelling word that matches the definition.

11. To bother someone _____

12. To rebound after hitting something _____

13. To stay clear of _____

14. A part of speech that names a person, place, or thing _____

15. To provide with paying work _____

Challenge Extension: Have students write dictionary definitions of the Challenge Words. Then exchange with a partner and write the Challenge Words that match each other's definitions.

Grade 4/Unit 3
The Hatmaker's Sign 15

Words with /ou/ and /oi/

Proofreading Activity

There are 6 spelling mistakes in the paragraph below. Circle the misspelled words. Write the words correctly on the lines below.

Benjamin Franklin was an interesting man. He was comfortable with common men and roialty. He liked to take walks arownd Philadelphia, and was always on the lookouwt for ways to improve the city. He invented things for his own enjoiment. He was never known to avoyd a problem or task. Ben would not disappoynt a friend in need.

1. _____   3. _____   5. _____

2. _____   4. _____   6. _____

Writing Activity

Do you have a favorite person from history? Write something you think that person might say if he or she were alive today, using four spelling words.

_____

_____

_____

_____

Words with /ou/ and /oi/

Look at the words in each set below. One word in each set is spelled correctly. Use a pencil to fill in the circle next to the correct word. Before you begin, look at the sample sets of words. Sample A has been done for you. Do Sample B by yourself. When you are sure you know what to do, you may go on with the rest of the page.

Sample A
Ⓐ broun
Ⓑ broin
Ⓒ brown
Ⓓ brouwn

Sample B
Ⓔ coin
Ⓕ coyne
Ⓖ coien
Ⓗ coyen

1.
Ⓐ oilee
Ⓑ oyly
Ⓒ oily
Ⓓ oiyle

2.
Ⓔ anoy
Ⓕ annoy
Ⓖ annoie
Ⓗ anoiy

3.
Ⓐ uround
Ⓑ around
Ⓒ arrownd
Ⓓ arowund

4.
Ⓔ groul
Ⓕ graul
Ⓖ growl
Ⓗ garowl

5.
Ⓐ dissapoint
Ⓑ disappoynte
Ⓒ disapoynt
Ⓓ disappoint

6.
Ⓔ royalty
Ⓕ royltie
Ⓖ roialty
Ⓗ royelty

7.
Ⓐ bounce
Ⓑ bownse
Ⓒ bounz
Ⓓ bouwnse

8.
Ⓔ bouing
Ⓕ bowing
Ⓖ bowwing
Ⓗ bowung

9.
Ⓐ moiste
Ⓑ moist
Ⓒ moyst
Ⓓ mosit

10.
Ⓔ enjoymant
Ⓕ enjoiment
Ⓖ anjoymint
Ⓗ enjoyment

11.
Ⓐ elloud
Ⓑ alowud
Ⓒ aloud
Ⓓ iloud

12.
Ⓔ towir
Ⓕ touer
Ⓖ tower
Ⓗ twore

13.
Ⓐ avoid
Ⓑ ivoid
Ⓒ avoyd
Ⓓ ahvoid

14.
Ⓔ employ
Ⓕ emploiy
Ⓖ imploy
Ⓗ amploi

15.
Ⓐ lookowt
Ⓑ lokout
Ⓒ lokowut
Ⓓ lookout

16.
Ⓔ howavir
Ⓕ halevere
Ⓖ hilever
Ⓗ however

17.
Ⓐ apoyntment
Ⓑ appointment
Ⓒ upointmant
Ⓓ ipointment

18.
Ⓔ skowt
Ⓕ scout
Ⓖ scault
Ⓗ scoit

19.
Ⓐ palder
Ⓑ podre
Ⓒ powder
Ⓓ powdor

20.
Ⓔ naln
Ⓕ nown
Ⓖ noun
Ⓗ noune

Words with /u̇/ and /yu̇/

Pretest Directions

Fold back the paper along the dotted line. Use the blanks to write each word as it is read aloud. When you finish the test, unfold the paper. Use the list at the right to correct any spelling mistakes. Practice the words that you missed for the Posttest.

To Parents

Here are the results of your child's weekly spelling Pretest. You can help your child study for the Posttest by following these simple steps for each word on the list:

1. Read the word to your child.

2. Have your child write the word, saying each letter as it is written.

3. Say each letter of the word as your child checks the spelling.

4. If a mistake has been made, have your child read each letter of the correctly spelled word aloud, then repeat steps 1–3.

1. _____	1. curious
2. _____	2. pure
3. _____	3. fully
4. _____	4. sure
5. _____	5. wooden
6. _____	6. should
7. _____	7. furious
8. _____	8. cure
9. _____	9. handful
10. _____	10. crooked
11. _____	11. would
12. _____	12. bulldozer
13. _____	13. soot
14. _____	14. tour
15. _____	15. butcher
16. _____	16. woolen
17. _____	17. pudding
18. _____	18. goodness
19. _____	19. pulley
20. _____	20. overlook

Challenge Words

_____ exist

_____ image

_____ inspire

_____ reference

_____ sketch

Words with /u̇/ and /yu̇/

Using the Word Study Steps

1. LOOK at the word.

2. SAY the word aloud.

3. STUDY the letters in the word.

4. WRITE the word.

5. CHECK the word.

   Did you spell the word right? If not, go back to step 1.

Spelling Tip

Words with a vowel sound as in the word *fully* are often spelled with *u*.
(butcher, handful)

Words with a vowel sound as in the word *wooden* are often spelled with *oo*.
(crooked, woolen)

Find and Circle

Where are the spelling words?

```
pfuriouszakbulldozervbdbntoherxxgoodness

uwfullyopclwoodenrlstovldrrsootuucurexxzz

rqvtoursuregspuremubutcherwwhandfulyyre

epulleyzacuriouseardlulrpuddinguucrooked

boverlookexdwouldbnewoolenuushouldaabb
```

To Parents or Helpers

   Using the Word Study Steps above as your child comes across any new words will help him or her learn to spell words effectively. Review the steps as you both go over this week's spelling words.

   Go over each Spelling Tip with your child. Ask your child to find other spelling words spelled with u and oo that sound like fully and wooden.

   Help your child complete the spelling activity.

Words with /ů/ and /yů/

curious	wooden	handful	soot	pudding
pure	should	crooked	tour	goodness
fully	furious	would	butcher	pulley
sure	cure	bulldozer	woolen	overlook

Pattern Power!

Write the spelling words with these spelling patterns.

Words with /yů/ spelled

u

1. _____

2. _____

u-e

3. _____

4. _____

Words with /ů/ spelled

u

5. _____

6. _____

7. _____

8. _____

9. _____

10. _____

Words with /ů/ spelled

u-e

11. _____

oo

12. _____

13. _____

14. _____

15. _____

16. _____

17. _____

ou

18. _____

19. _____

20. _____

Words with /u̇/ and /yu̇/

curious	wooden	handful	soot	pudding
pure	should	crooked	tour	goodness
fully	furious	would	butcher	pulley
sure	cure	bulldozer	woolen	overlook

Definitions for You

Fill in the word from the spelling list that matches the definition.

1. made from the hair of sheep _____

2. interested in learning more _____

3. to fail to notice _____

4. free of dirt or pollution _____

5. made from trees _____

6. a word used to express duty _____

7. having bends or curves _____

8. the amount a hand can hold _____

9. black particles left after wood or coal are burned _____

10. completely or totally _____

11. a word used to make a polite request _____

12. desirable qualities _____

13. a method that brings back health _____

14. impossible to doubt _____

15. to be very angry _____

16. a creamy dessert _____

Challenge Extension: Pair up students. Have one partner use the dictionary to write short definitions for each Challenge Word. Then let the other partner use the definitions to make up one sentence for each

Grade 4/Unit 3

Pat Cummings: My Story `16`

Words with /ů/ and /yů/

Proofreading Activity

There are six spelling mistakes in the paragraph. Circle the misspelled words.
Write the words correctly on the lines below.

     Last fall I went to the community crafts fair and saw lots of interesting
things. One woman was making old-fashioned wudden toys from pieces of pine
and maple. I bought a buledozer that really works for my little brother. A
candlemaker was selling candles made from pur beeswax. A weaver was making
beautiful wollen shawls and scarves. I bought a handfool of bright, shiny marbles.
I got cyrious when I saw a crowd of people gathered in a circle. When I got closer
I saw someone making blown glass animals. It was a fun day.

1. _____   3. _____   5. _____

2. _____   4. _____   6. _____

Writing Activity

Using four spelling words, describe a crafts fair or other festival that you have
attended.

_____

_____

_____

_____

Words with /u̇/ and /yu̇/

Look at the words in each set below. One word in each set is spelled correctly. Use a pencil to fill in the circle next to the correct word. Before you begin, look at the sample sets of words. Sample A has been done for you. Do Sample B by yourself. When you are sure you know what to do, you may go on with the rest of the page.

Sample A
- (A) poor ●
- (B) puer
- (C) por
- (D) puore

Sample B
- (E) coulde
- (F) could
- (G) kould
- (H) cuold

1.
- (A) overloke
- (B) ovirlook
- (C) overlook
- (D) ovarlouk

2.
- (E) puley
- (F) pullie
- (G) pouley
- (H) pulley

3.
- (A) gudness
- (B) goodness
- (C) goodnis
- (D) goudness

4.
- (E) pulding
- (F) pudden
- (G) pudding
- (H) pooding

5.
- (A) woolen
- (B) wulen
- (C) woolin
- (D) woulen

6.
- (E) bucher
- (F) butcher
- (G) bootcher
- (H) butsher

7.
- (A) tour
- (B) toor
- (C) ture
- (D) tuyre

8.
- (E) soot
- (F) sut
- (G) soote
- (H) soute

9.
- (A) booldoxer
- (B) bulldoxer
- (C) buldozar
- (D) bulldozer

10.
- (E) wuld
- (F) wolde
- (G) would
- (H) woold

11.
- (A) krooked
- (B) crooked
- (C) crookad
- (D) crucked

12.
- (E) handful
- (F) hanfull
- (G) handfool
- (H) hannful

13.
- (A) cyure
- (B) coure
- (C) cure
- (D) ciure

14.
- (E) fureus
- (F) furrius
- (G) furious
- (H) farious

15.
- (A) should
- (B) sould
- (C) shuuld
- (D) shold

16.
- (E) wooden
- (F) wuden
- (G) woodan
- (H) wouldin

17.
- (A) soore
- (B) sure
- (C) suyre
- (D) soure

18.
- (E) fulie
- (F) fully
- (G) fooly
- (H) fullyie

19.
- (A) puyre
- (B) poour
- (C) pure
- (D) puare

20.
- (E) cureus
- (F) kurious
- (G) karius
- (H) curious

Grade 4/Unit 3
Pat Cummings: My Story
20

Words with Digraphs

Fold back the paper along the dotted line. Use the blanks to write each word as it is read aloud. When you finish the test, unfold the paper. Use the list at the right to correct any spelling mistakes. Practice the words you missed for the Posttest.

To Parents
Here are the results of your child's weekly spelling Pretest. You can help your child study for the Posttest by following these simple steps for each word on the word list:

1. Read the word to your child.

2. Have your child write the word, saying each letter as it is written.

3. Say each letter of the word as your child checks the spelling.

4. If a mistake has been made, have your child read each letter of the correctly spelled word aloud, then repeat steps 1–3.

1. _____ 1. changed
2. _____ 2. watch
3. _____ 3. fresh
4. _____ 4. shoulder
5. _____ 5. whatever
6. _____ 6. south
7. _____ 7. chimney
8. _____ 8. scratch
9. _____ 9. shove
10. _____ 10. wheat
11. _____ 11. cloth
12. _____ 12. themselves
13. _____ 13. crunch
14. _____ 14. batch
15. _____ 15. harsh
16. _____ 16. whittle
17. _____ 17. thoughtful
18. _____ 18. birch
19. _____ 19. switch
20. _____ 20. theater

Challenge Words

_____ chanted
_____ pouch
_____ restless
_____ scribbled
_____ stitching

Words with Digraphs

Using the Word Study Steps

1. LOOK at the word.
2. SAY the word aloud.
3. STUDY the letters in the word.
4. WRITE the word.
5. CHECK the word.

   Did you spell the word right? If not, go back to step 1.

Spelling Tip

If the /ch/ immediately follows a short vowel in a one-syllable word, it is spelled *tch*: *watch*, *scratch*.

There are a few exceptions in English: *much*, *such*, *which*, and *rich*.

Word Scramble

1. hctarcs _____
2. veslesmeht _____
3. hruncc _____
4. htolc _____
5. hhsra _____
6. hctba _____
7. denaghc _____
8. veretahw _____
9. houts _____
10. aethw _____

11. hrcib _____
12. hcawt _____
13. hsrfe _____
14. lreduohs _____
15. eymnich _____
16. voehs _____
17. teltihw _____
18. lutfhgouht _____
19. thciws _____
20. taehtre _____

To Parents or Helpers

Using the Word Study Steps above as your child comes across any new words will help him or her learn to spell words effectively. Review the steps as you both go over this week's spelling words.

Go over each Spelling Tip with your child. Help your child find other spelling words spelled with *tch*.

Help your child complete the spelling activity.

Grade 4/Unit 3
Grass Sandals `20`

Words with Digraphs

changed	whatever	shove	crunch	thoughtful
watch	south	wheat	batch	birch
fresh	chimney	cloth	harsh	switch
shoulder	scratch	themselves	whittle	theater

Pattern Power
Write the words that have these spelling patterns.

ch

1. _____
2. _____
3. _____
4. _____

tch

5. _____
6. _____
7. _____
8. _____

th

9. _____
10. _____
11. _____
12. _____
13. _____

sh

14. _____
15. _____
16. _____
17. _____

wh

18. _____
19. _____
20. _____

Words with Digraphs

changed	whatever	shove	crunch	thoughtful
watch	south	wheat	batch	birch
fresh	chimney	cloth	harsh	switch
shoulder	scratch	themselves	whittle	theater

What's the Word?

Complete each sentence with a spelling word.

1. Would you like to _____ the parade with me?

2. My aunt likes to _____ small figures from tree branches.

3. Young children like to do things by _____.

4. During free time, we can do _____ we want.

5. He hurt his _____ when he threw the ball too hard.

6. The _____ tree has a pretty, white bark.

7. The smoke from the fireplace goes up the _____.

8. We may have to _____ the stuck door to open it.

9. The midwestern states grow a lot of _____.

10. I'm going to the _____ on Friday to see a play.

Just the Opposite

Write a word from the spelling list that has the opposite meaning from the word or phrase below.

11. stayed the same   _____

12. stale   _____

13. north   _____

14. mild   _____

15. a single one   _____

Challenge Extension: Have students write a "fill-in-the-blank" sentence for each Challenge Word and then exchange papers with a partner to complete each other's sentences.

Grade 4/Unit 3
Grass Sandals   15

Name_____ Date_____

Words with Digraphs

Proofreading Activity

There are 6 spelling mistakes in the paragraph. Circle the misspelled words.
Write the words correctly on the lines below.

My uncle has always enjoyed working with wood. He says it gives him time
to be quiet and thotfull. I like to wach him while he works. He likes to witle small
birds and forest animals from pieces of wood that he finds on his hikes. His
favorite wood to use is bersh. He uses sandpaper to make the wood smooth, so
it won't skracth him. Then he carefully uses a knife to make the shape of the
animal. The first time I saw a piece of wood shanjed into a real-looking rabbit, I
was amazed.

1. _____ 3. _____ 5. _____

2. _____ 4. _____ 6. _____

Writing Activity

Write a paragraph about something you like to make. Use four words from your
spelling list.

_____

_____

_____

_____

Words with Digraphs

Look at the words in each set below. One word in each set is spelled correctly. Use a pencil to fill in the circle next to the correct word. Before you begin, look at the sample sets of words. Sample A has been done for you. Do Sample B by yourself. When you are sure you know what to do, you may go on with the rest of the page.

Sample A
- Ⓐ matsh
- Ⓑ macht
- ● match
- Ⓓ matsch

Sample B
- Ⓔ ship
- Ⓕ sheip
- Ⓖ shyip
- Ⓗ shiip

1.
- Ⓐ wehat
- Ⓑ weet
- Ⓒ wheat
- Ⓓ hweat

6.
- Ⓔ crounch
- Ⓕ crunch
- Ⓖ krunch
- Ⓗ cruntch

11.
- Ⓐ shuv
- Ⓑ chove
- Ⓒ shove
- Ⓓ schuve

16.
- Ⓔ sawitch
- Ⓕ switch
- Ⓖ swithc
- Ⓗ siwatch

2.
- Ⓔ kloth
- Ⓕ clotsh
- Ⓖ cloth
- Ⓗ cloath

7.
- Ⓐ barsh
- Ⓑ birch
- Ⓒ birtch
- Ⓓ bersh

12.
- Ⓔ toutful
- Ⓕ tehoughtful
- Ⓖ thoughtful
- Ⓗ thougtfill

17.
- Ⓐ wathc
- Ⓑ watch
- Ⓒ wetch
- Ⓓ wahtc

3.
- Ⓐ thamselvs
- Ⓑ thimsilves
- Ⓒ temmselves
- Ⓓ themselves

8.
- Ⓔ faresh
- Ⓕ fretch
- Ⓖ freetsh
- Ⓗ fresh

13.
- Ⓐ harsh
- Ⓑ hartch
- Ⓒ harrsh
- Ⓓ harss

18.
- Ⓔ south
- Ⓕ salth
- Ⓖ souhh
- Ⓗ sotch

4.
- Ⓔ changed
- Ⓕ shanged
- Ⓖ cahnged
- Ⓗ schanged

9.
- Ⓐ whutevir
- Ⓑ watevver
- Ⓒ wahtever
- Ⓓ whatever

14.
- Ⓔ skratch
- Ⓕ scrith
- Ⓖ scaracih
- Ⓗ scratch

19.
- Ⓐ whittle
- Ⓑ wuhittle
- Ⓒ hwittel
- Ⓓ whotel

5.
- Ⓐ theater
- Ⓑ theeter
- Ⓒ tcheater
- Ⓓ tsheater

10.
- Ⓔ chiminey
- Ⓕ chimney
- Ⓖ shimmney
- Ⓗ shemnie

15.
- Ⓐ chulder
- Ⓑ shoulder
- Ⓒ sahoulder
- Ⓓ thoulder

20.
- Ⓔ batach
- Ⓕ basth
- Ⓖ bocht
- Ⓗ batch

Adding *-ed* and *-ing*

Fold back the paper along the dotted line. Use the blanks to write each word as it is read aloud. When you finish the test, unfold the paper. Use the list at the right to correct any spelling mistakes. Practice the words you missed for the Posttest.

To Parents
Here are the results of your child's weekly spelling Pretest. You can help your child study for the Posttest by following these simple steps for each word on the word list:

1. Read the word to your child.

2. Have your child write the word, saying each letter as it is written.

3. Say each letter of the word as your child checks the spelling.

4. If a mistake has been made, have your child read each letter of the correctly spelled word aloud, then repeat steps 1–3.

1. _____ 1. freed
2. _____ 2. hugged
3. _____ 3. emptied
4. _____ 4. figured
5. _____ 5. budding
6. _____ 6. carried
7. _____ 7. believed
8. _____ 8. dimmed
9. _____ 9. studied
10. _____ 10. providing
11. _____ 11. shedding
12. _____ 12. sledding
13. _____ 13. magnified
14. _____ 14. wedged
15. _____ 15. rotting
16. _____ 16. varied
17. _____ 17. arrived
18. _____ 18. plugging
19. _____ 19. rising
20. _____ 20. celebrated

Challenge Words

_____ fretted
_____ gourd
_____ plantation
_____ settlement
_____ sunrise

Adding *-ed* and *-ing*

Using the Word Study Steps

1. LOOK at the word.

2. SAY the word aloud.

3. STUDY the letters in the word.

4. WRITE the word.

5. CHECK the word.

Did you spell the word right?
If not, go back to step 1.

Spelling Tip

When words end in silent *e*, drop the *e* when adding an ending that begins with a vowel.
believe - e + ing = believing

When a one syllable word ends in one vowel followed by one consonant, double the consonant before adding an ending that begins with a vowel.
hug + ed = hugged

When a word ends with a consonant followed by *y*, change the *y* to *i* when adding any ending except endings that begin with *i*.
empty + ed = emptied

Word Endings

Write the spelling word by crossing off the final -e and then adding *-ed* or *-ing*.

1. free _____

2. believe _____

3. figure _____

4. arrive _____

5. rise _____

6. celebrate _____

7. provide _____

8. wedge _____

Write the spelling word by doubling the final consonant and adding *-ed* or *-ing*.

9. hug _____

10. bud _____

11. dim _____

12. shed_____

Write the spelling word by changing *y* to *i* and then adding *-ed*.

13. empty_____

14. carry _____

15. study _____

16. vary _____

To Parents or Helpers

Using the Word Study Steps above as your child comes across any new words will help him or her learn to spell words effectively. Review the steps as you both go over this week's spelling words.

Go over each Spelling Tip with your child. Ask him or her to add -s or -es to form plurals. Ask if he or she knows other words that end with a consonant followed by y. Help your child to use the Spelling Tips to add endings to the words to make them plural.

Help your child complete the spelling activity.

Adding *-ed* and *-ing*

freed	budding	studied	magnified	arrived
hugged	carried	providing	wedged	plugging
emptied	believed	shedding	rotting	rising
figured	dimmed	sledding	varied	celebrated

Pattern Power

Write the spelling words that double the consonant before adding *-ed*.

1. _____ 2. _____

Write the spelling words that drop the *e* before adding *-ed*.

3. _____ 4. _____ 5. _____

6. _____ 7. _____ 8. _____

Write the spelling words that change *y* to *i* before adding *-ed*.

9. _____ 10. _____ 11. _____

12. _____ 13. _____

Write the spelling words that double the consonant before adding *-ing*.

14. _____ 15. _____ 16. _____

17. _____ 18. _____

Write the spelling words that drop the *e* before adding *-ing*.

19. _____ 20. _____

Adding *-ed* and *-ing*

freed	budding	studied	magnified	arrived
hugged	carried	providing	wedged	plugging
emptied	believed	shedding	rotting	rising
figured	dimmed	sledding	varied	celebrated

Fill in the Blanks

Complete each sentence with a word from the spelling list.

1. Last year we _____ the Fourth of July with fireworks.

2. Which do you like better, ice skating or _____?

3. We'll start the night hike when the moon is _____.

4. My cousins _____ just in time for the party.

5. The tiny insects were _____ by the microscope.

6. My dog is messy when he starts _____ his hair!

7. I got an A on the test because I _____ hard.

8. The plants began _____ when spring arrived.

9. The coach _____ our routines so we wouldn't get bored.

10. Our team _____ out the answer first.

What Does It Mean?

Write the base word for each spelling word.

11. freed _____

12. hugged _____

13. emptied _____

14. carried _____

15. believed _____

16. dimmed _____

17. providing _____

18. wedged _____

19. rotting _____

20. plugging _____

Challenge Extension: Have students create a crossword puzzle using the Challenge Words, then work with a partner to complete each other's sentences.

Adding *-ed* and *-ing*

Proofreading Activity

There are 6 spelling mistakes in the paragraph. Circle the misspelled words.
Write the words correctly on the lines below.

     Last week we celebrat my dad's birthday with a surprise party. All of our
relatives and friends met at our favorite restaurant. Around 5:30, my brothers
caryed in the presents. The other guests were already there, all hiding in corners
and behind chairs. The lights were dimned. I arryved with my dad around 6
o'clock. My mom turned up the lights. Then everyone stood up and shouted
"Happy Birthday, Mike!" My dad was so happy, he huged us all. He said we really
tricked him; he believeed my story about going to a soccer dinner. It was a great
party. I wonder what we'll think of for next year!

1. _____   3. _____   5. _____

2. _____   4. _____   6. _____

Writing Activity

Write about a celebration you had. Use at least four spelling words in your
description.

_____

_____

_____

_____

Adding *-ed* and *-ing*

Look at the words in each set below. One word in each set is spelled correctly. Use a pencil to fill in the circle next to the correct word. Before you begin, look at the sample sets of words. Sample A has been done for you. Do Sample B by yourself. When you are sure you know what to do, you may go on with the rest of the page.

Sample A
(A) cryed
(B) cried
(C) cryied
(D) cride

Sample B
(E) swiming
(F) swimmen
(G) swimming
(H) swiminng

1. (A) studdide
   (B) studyed
   (C) studdied
   (D) studied

2. (E) carryed
   (F) carrid
   (G) caried
   (H) carried

3. (A) arived
   (B) arrived
   (C) arryved
   (D) arrivde

4. (E) riseing
   (F) rising
   (G) rissing
   (H) risseng

5. (A) figureed
   (B) figgured
   (C) figured
   (D) figurrid

6. (E) roting
   (F) rotteing
   (G) rotenng
   (H) rotting

7. (A) vairied
   (B) varied
   (C) varyd
   (D) variyd

8. (E) freed
   (F) fereed
   (G) frede
   (H) fread

9. (A) sleden
   (B) sledding
   (C) sledinng
   (D) sleading

10. (E) hugedd
    (F) hugged
    (G) huggid
    (H) hugded

11. (A) celebrated
    (B) celebarated
    (C) celibratid
    (D) celebratde

12. (E) pluging
    (F) pluuging
    (G) puluging
    (H) plugging

13. (A) maganified
    (B) magnified
    (C) magnifyde
    (D) magnafide

14. (E) buhding
    (F) budeing
    (G) budding
    (H) buddeng

15. (A) dimend
    (B) dimned
    (C) dimede
    (D) dimmed

16. (E) provideing
    (F) providing
    (G) providding
    (H) prooviding

17. (A) sheading
    (B) shedeng
    (C) shedding
    (D) shedeing

18. (E) weged
    (F) wedgded
    (G) wedged
    (H) wejde

19. (A) believed
    (B) bulieved
    (C) baleeved
    (D) beleiveed

20. (E) emptied
    (F) emted
    (G) empttied
    (H) emptyed

Words from the Arts

Fold back the paper along the dotted line. Use the blanks to write each word as it is read aloud. When you finish the test, unfold the paper. Use the list at the right to correct any spelling mistakes. Practice the words you missed for the Posttest.

To Parents
Here are the results of your child's weekly spelling Pretest. You can help your child study for the Posttest by following these simple steps for each word on the word list:

1. Read the word to your child.

2. Have your child write the word, saying each letter as it is written.

3. Say each letter of the word as your child checks the spelling.

4. If a mistake has been made, have your child read each letter of the correctly spelled word aloud, then repeat steps 1–3.

1. _____	1. designs
2. _____	2. artist
3. _____	3. building
4. _____	4. activity
5. _____	5. museum
6. _____	6. art
7. _____	7. create
8. _____	8. master
9. _____	9. poster
10. _____	10. statue
11. _____	11. assemble
12. _____	12. craft
13. _____	13. express
14. _____	14. arrange
15. _____	15. professional
16. _____	16. mold
17. _____	17. easel
18. _____	18. plaster
19. _____	19. masterpiece
20. _____	20. exhibit

Challenge Words

_____	challenge
_____	contained
_____	entertaining
_____	mazes
_____	requires

Words from the Arts

Using the Word Study Steps

1. LOOK at the word.

2. SAY the word aloud.

3. STUDY the letters in the word.

4. WRITE the word.

5. CHECK the word.

   Did you spell the word right?
   If not, go back to step 1.

Spelling Tip
   Look for word chunks or smaller words that help you remember the spelling of a word.

assemble = as sem ble
professional = pro fes sion al
masterpiece = mas ter piece

Word Scramble

Unscramble each set of letters to make a spelling word.

1. tyiavcit _____

2. srofeasipnlo _____

3. ateemriscep _____

4. starti _____

5. beamsles _____

6. srespex _____

7. frtca _____

8. rateec _____

9. sotepr _____

10. alsee _____

11. sigends _____

12. gudilibn _____

13. smarte _____

14. geararn _____

15. doml _____

16. xeitbih _____

17. parstel _____

18. rat _____

19. umusme _____

20. usteat _____

To Parents or Helpers
   Using the Word Study Steps above as your child comes across any new words will help him or her learn to spell words effectively. Review the steps as you both go over this week's spelling words.
   Go over the Spelling Tip with your child. Help your child find the smaller words within the spelling words.
   Help your child complete the spelling activity.

Words from the Arts

designs	museum	poster	express	easel
artist	art	statue	arrange	plaster
building	create	assemble	professional	masterpiece
activity	master	craft	mold	exhibit

Write the spelling words in alphabetical order.

1. _____   11. _____

2. _____   12. _____

3. _____   13. _____

4. _____   14. _____

5. _____   15. _____

6. _____   16. _____

7. _____   17. _____

8. _____   18. _____

9. _____   19. _____

10. _____   20. _____

Words from the Arts

designs	museum	poster	express	easel
artist	art	statue	arrange	plaster
building	create	assemble	professional	masterpiece
activity	master	craft	mold	exhibit

What is the Meaning?

Find the word from the spelling list that matches each definition below.

1. someone who earns a living in an occupation _____

2. a public showing _____

3. something made by skilled hands _____

4. a container used to make shapes _____

5. a structure with walls and a roof _____

6. a sticky substance used by builders _____

7. decorative patterns _____

8. to make something _____

What's the Word?

Complete each sentence with a spelling word.

9. Can you _____ the books neatly on the shelf?

10. It's a challenge to _____ this 500-piece jigsaw puzzle.

11. I study painting with a talented _____ teacher.

12. Last week I made a _____ to advertise the school play.

13. That _____ of a boy is so lifelike, it looks real.

14. We were busy at camp doing one _____ after another.

15. Do you like to _____ yourself through writing or drawing?

16. I saw a great _____ at the museum the other day.

Challenge Extension: Write the Challenge Words on the board in scrambled order and ask students to write them in alphabetical order.

Words from the Arts

Proofreading Activity

There are 6 spelling mistakes in the directions below. Circle the misspelled words. Write the words correctly on the lines below.

Getting Ready to Paint a Picture

1. Think about the feeling or idea you want to ecspress in your painting.

2. Assembal all of your equipment.

3. Sketch several desins on paper first.

4. Arange your brushes and paints so they are easy to reach.

5. Put a blank canvas on an esel.

6. Use your brushes, paints, and ideas to creight a wonderful painting.

1. _____   3. _____   5. _____

2. _____   4. _____   6. _____

Writing Activity

Write a set of directions telling how to do something artistic. Number each step. Use at least four spelling words.

_____

_____

_____

_____

_____

Words from the Arts

Look at the words in each set below. One word in each set is spelled correctly. Use a pencil to fill in the circle next to the correct word. Before you begin, look at the sample sets of words. Sample A has been done for you. Do Sample B by yourself. When you are sure you know what to do, you may go on with the rest of the page.

Sample A
- Ⓐ burush
- Ⓑ bruch
- Ⓒ baruch
- Ⓓ brush

Sample B
- Ⓔ canvas
- Ⓕ canvis
- Ⓖ kanvas
- Ⓗ kanvist

1.
- Ⓐ activity
- Ⓑ acativety
- Ⓒ acktvity
- Ⓓ actevaty

2.
- Ⓔ statoo
- Ⓕ statue
- Ⓖ satatue
- Ⓗ statshoo

3.
- Ⓐ deesines
- Ⓑ desighns
- Ⓒ designs
- Ⓓ desines

4.
- Ⓔ crafet
- Ⓕ caraft
- Ⓖ curaft
- Ⓗ craft

5.
- Ⓐ plastar
- Ⓑ plaster
- Ⓒ plasstir
- Ⓓ pullaster

6.
- Ⓔ masterpieace
- Ⓕ masterrpece
- Ⓖ masterpiece
- Ⓗ mazzterpiece

7.
- Ⓐ artest
- Ⓑ artist
- Ⓒ ardizt
- Ⓓ ahrtist

8.
- Ⓔ prufesionel
- Ⓕ proffesional
- Ⓖ prifesionul
- Ⓗ professional

9.
- Ⓐ create
- Ⓑ kreatee
- Ⓒ creeate
- Ⓓ chreat

10.
- Ⓔ ixpress
- Ⓕ express
- Ⓖ ackspres
- Ⓗ egspress

11.
- Ⓐ urange
- Ⓑ arannge
- Ⓒ araange
- Ⓓ arrange

12.
- Ⓔ poster
- Ⓕ poaster
- Ⓖ postear
- Ⓗ puhster

13.
- Ⓐ ezel
- Ⓑ easel
- Ⓒ eesil
- Ⓓ easile

14.
- Ⓔ ahrt
- Ⓕ arrt
- Ⓖ artte
- Ⓗ art

15.
- Ⓐ ecksibit
- Ⓑ eaxibet
- Ⓒ exhibit
- Ⓓ egsebet

16.
- Ⓔ asembal
- Ⓕ assemble
- Ⓖ usembul
- Ⓗ asemmbale

17.
- Ⓐ moseim
- Ⓑ mahuseem
- Ⓒ muzeume
- Ⓓ museum

18.
- Ⓔ masster
- Ⓕ mastear
- Ⓖ master
- Ⓗ mostare

19.
- Ⓐ buldding
- Ⓑ bildeng
- Ⓒ building
- Ⓓ biuldang

20.
- Ⓔ mold
- Ⓕ moald
- Ⓖ muold
- Ⓗ mollde

Grade 4/Unit 3 Review Test

Read each sentence. If an underlined word is spelled wrong, fill in the circle that
goes with that word. If no word is spelled wrong, fill in the circle below NONE.
Read Sample A, and do Sample B.

A. That <u>artist</u> made colorful <u>designs</u> on her <u>poster</u>.
     A   B   C

NONE
A. Ⓐ Ⓑ Ⓒ ●

B. The <u>plaster</u> isn't <u>moyst</u> enough to pour into the <u>mold</u>.
     E   F   G

NONE
B. Ⓔ Ⓕ Ⓖ Ⓗ

1. Use <u>powder</u> to <u>avoid</u> <u>ouly</u> skin.
      A   B   C

NONE
1. Ⓐ Ⓑ Ⓒ Ⓓ

2. The <u>museum</u> <u>exibit</u> included a <u>pulley</u>.
     E   F   G

NONE
2. Ⓔ Ⓕ Ⓖ Ⓗ

3. It's <u>curious</u> to see <u>royalty</u> bounce their <u>checks</u>.
      A   B   C

NONE
3. Ⓐ Ⓑ Ⓒ Ⓓ

4. The <u>pure</u> marble <u>statchew</u> is a <u>masterpiece</u>.
     E   F   G

NONE
4. Ⓔ Ⓕ Ⓖ Ⓗ

5. The <u>professional</u> had <u>soot</u> <u>wedjed</u> into his collar.
        A   B   C

NONE
5. Ⓐ Ⓑ Ⓒ Ⓓ

6. The <u>tour</u> guide led us to the <u>museeum</u> <u>exhibit</u>.
     E   F   G

NONE
6. Ⓔ Ⓕ Ⓖ Ⓗ

7. The <u>crunsh</u> of the <u>rotting</u> apple had a <u>harsh</u> sound.
      A   B   C

NONE
7. Ⓐ Ⓑ Ⓒ Ⓓ

8. Try to <u>avoyd</u> mixing <u>rotting</u> fruit in the <u>batch</u>.
        E   F   G

NONE
8. Ⓔ Ⓕ Ⓖ Ⓗ

9. I can <u>whittle</u> <u>curious</u> designs and have them <u>magnifyed</u>.
       A   B   C

NONE
9. Ⓐ Ⓑ Ⓒ Ⓓ

10. On a <u>tour</u> of the <u>theater</u> I saw seating for <u>royalte</u>.
      E   F   G

NONE
10. Ⓔ Ⓕ Ⓖ Ⓗ

11. <u>Freed</u> prisoners <u>emptied</u> their cells in the <u>harsh</u> jail.
     A   B   C

NONE
11. Ⓐ Ⓑ Ⓒ Ⓓ

Grade 4/Unit 3 Review Test

12. He <u>emptyed</u> an account to <u>avoid</u> having a check <u>bounce</u>.
    E   F   G
12. Ⓔ Ⓕ Ⓖ Ⓗ NONE

13. We will <u>powdir</u> the <u>batch</u> of cookies with <u>pure</u> sugar.
    A   B   C
13. Ⓐ Ⓑ Ⓒ Ⓓ NONE

14. During the <u>theatir</u> <u>tour</u>, they will use a <u>pulley</u>.
    E   F   G
14. Ⓔ Ⓕ Ⓖ Ⓗ NONE

15. He will <u>wittle</u> a wood <u>statue</u> and give it to <u>royalty</u>.
    A   B   C
15. Ⓐ Ⓑ Ⓒ Ⓓ NONE

16. The <u>soot</u> looks like <u>powder</u> when <u>magnified</u>.
    E   F   G
16. Ⓔ Ⓕ Ⓖ Ⓗ NONE

17. The <u>professional</u> <u>freed</u> up his time for a <u>masterpeice</u>.
    A   B   C
17. Ⓐ Ⓑ Ⓒ Ⓓ NONE

18. He <u>wedged</u> the <u>roting</u> <u>oily</u> board in the corner.
    E   F   G
18. Ⓔ Ⓕ Ⓖ Ⓗ NONE

19. The <u>crunch</u> became <u>magnified</u> with each dropped <u>bache</u>.
    A   B   C
19. Ⓐ Ⓑ Ⓒ Ⓓ NONE

20. A <u>profesional</u> will set up the <u>museum</u> <u>exhibit</u>.
    E   F   G
20. Ⓔ Ⓕ Ⓖ Ⓗ NONE

21. The <u>statue</u> in the <u>theater</u> is a <u>masterpiece</u>.
    A   B   C
21. Ⓐ Ⓑ Ⓒ Ⓓ NONE

22. He would <u>whittle</u> the <u>wedged</u> stick until he was <u>freeed</u>.
    E   F   G
22. Ⓔ Ⓕ Ⓖ Ⓗ NONE

23. She heard a <u>harsh</u> <u>crunch</u> and a <u>cureous</u> bang.
    A   B   C
23. Ⓐ Ⓑ Ⓒ Ⓓ NONE

24. He <u>emptied</u> the box and saw a <u>pulley</u> <u>bounce</u> out.
    E   F   G
24. Ⓔ Ⓕ Ⓖ Ⓗ NONE

25. We saw <u>soot</u> and <u>oily</u> spots on the <u>pur</u> white floor.
    A   B   C
25. Ⓐ Ⓑ Ⓒ Ⓓ NONE

Name_____ Date_____

Words with /ô/ and /ôr/

Pretest Directions

Fold back the paper along the dotted line. Use the blanks to write each word as it is read aloud. When you finish the test, unfold the paper. Use the list at the right to correct any spelling mistakes. Practice the words you missed for the Posttest.

To Parents

Here are the results of your child's weekly spelling Pretest. You can help your child study for the Posttest by following these simple steps for each word on the word list:

1. Read the word to your child.

2. Have your child write the word, saying each letter as it is written.

3. Say each letter of the word as your child checks the spelling.

4. If a mistake has been made, have your child read each letter of the correctly spelled word aloud, and then repeat steps 1–3.

#		#	Word
1.	_____	1.	awful
2.	_____	2.	daughter
3.	_____	3.	roar
4.	_____	4.	order
5.	_____	5.	office
6.	_____	6.	toward
7.	_____	7.	already
8.	_____	8.	brought
9.	_____	9.	form
10.	_____	10.	author
11.	_____	11.	false
12.	_____	12.	jaw
13.	_____	13.	offer
14.	_____	14.	sauce
15.	_____	15.	chorus
16.	_____	16.	dawn
17.	_____	17.	hoarse
18.	_____	18.	war
19.	_____	19.	board
20.	_____	20.	cough

Challenge Words

_____ affection

_____ clinging

_____ methods

_____ threat

_____ injury

Words with /ô/ and /ôr/

Using the Word Study Steps

1. LOOK at the word.

2. SAY the word aloud.

3. STUDY the letters in the word.

4. WRITE the word.

5. CHECK the word.

   Did you spell the word right?
   If not, go back to step 1.

Spelling Tip

Think of times you have read a word in a book, on a sign, or on a billboard. Try to remember how it looked. Then write the word in different ways. Which one looks correct?

ofice   oficce   office

Word Scramble

Unscramble each set of letters to make a spelling word.

1. wfaul _____

2. oghuc _____

3. morf _____

4. hutora _____

5. acesu _____

6. usorch _____

7. wand _____

8. rdtawo _____

9. aydreal _____

10. awj _____

11. rwa _____

12. ehsroa _____

13. rroa _____

14. bthgrou _____

15. dbroa _____

16. raedhtug _____

17. oedrr _____

18. ffore _____

19. sealf _____

20. ffecoi _____

To Parents or Helpers

Using the Word Study Steps above as your child comes across any new words will help him or her learn to spell words effectively. Review the steps as you both go over this week's spelling words.

Go over the Spelling Tip with your child. Help your child write some of the spelling words in different ways to figure out which one looks correct.

Help your child complete the spelling activity.

Words with /ô/ and /ôr/

awful	office	form	offer	hoarse
daughter	toward	author	sauce	war
roar	already	false	chorus	board
order	brought	jaw	dawn	cough

Word Sort
Write each spelling word under the matching vowel sound.

/ô/ spelled:

au

1. _____
2. _____

aw

3. _____
4. _____
5. _____

a

6. _____
7. _____

o

8. _____
9. _____

ough

10. _____
11. _____

augh

12. _____

/ôr/ spelled:

or

13. _____
14. _____
15. _____

oar

16. _____
17. _____
18. _____

ar

19. _____
20. _____

Words with /ô/ and /ôr/

awful	office	form	offer	hoarse
daughter	toward	author	sauce	war
roar	already	false	chorus	board
order	brought	jaw	dawn	cough

Use spelling words to complete the sentences below.

1. My _____ comes to visit me every week.

2. Cover your mouth when you _____, please.

3. His _____ was sore from chewing gum all day.

4. This _____ has ten computers and ten phones.

5. I have _____ finished my homework.

6. It is easy to find things that are placed in _____.

7. I was scared when the bear walked _____ me.

8. Did the nice lady _____ to carry the box?

9. The swimming pool is in the _____ of a rectangle.

10. Her voice sounds scratchy and _____ when she talks.

Definition Derby

Write the spelling word that matches each definition.

11. shout _____   16. battle _____

12. piece of wood _____   17. singers _____

13. carried _____   18. not true _____

14. gravy _____   19. daybreak _____

15. writer _____   20. terrible _____

Challenge Extension: Have students write a definition for any one of the Challenge Words on a piece of paper. Mix the papers in a box, inviting students to take turns picking and reading the definitions aloud. Let the class guess which Challenge Word fits each definition.

Words with /ô/ and /ôr/

Proofreading Activity

There are six spelling mistakes in this postcard. Circle the misspelled words. Write the words correctly on the lines below.

Dear Daughter,

  Daun is so beautiful in the Arctic! I allready had my camera out when I heard the scary and auful noise of a wolf pack. When a wolf ran toword me, I started snapping photos. I tried to ofer the wolf a piece of cheese to make him happy. He ate it up and wanted more. I'm glad I brouhgt extra cheese and film!

       Love,

       Father

1. _____ 3. _____ 5. _____

2. _____ 4. _____ 6. _____

Writing Activity

Pretend that you are a photo journalist exploring an exciting place, such as the Arctic. What do you think you would see, hear, and feel? Write a letter to a friend at home about your experience. Use four spelling words.

_____

_____

_____

_____

Words with /ô/ and /ôr/

Look at the words in each set below. One word in each set is spelled correctly. Use a pencil to fill in the circle next to the correct word. Before you begin, look at the sample sets of words. Sample A has been done for you. Do Sample B by yourself. When you are sure you know what to do, you may go on with the rest of the page.

Sample A
- Ⓐ sough
- Ⓑ saugh
- Ⓒ sau
- ⬤Ⓓ saw

Sample B
- Ⓔ stoarm
- Ⓕ storm
- Ⓖ starm
- Ⓗ storrm

1.
- Ⓐ ordr
- Ⓑ order
- Ⓒ oarder
- Ⓓ arder

6.
- Ⓔ dawn
- Ⓕ daun
- Ⓖ duan
- Ⓗ danw

11.
- Ⓐ faulse
- Ⓑ falsse
- Ⓒ fawlse
- Ⓓ false

16.
- Ⓔ burd
- Ⓕ baord
- Ⓖ boord
- Ⓗ board

2.
- Ⓔ athor
- Ⓕ auther
- Ⓖ authir
- Ⓗ author

7.
- Ⓐ sauce
- Ⓑ sace
- Ⓒ souce
- Ⓓ sause

12.
- Ⓔ hoarce
- Ⓕ hource
- Ⓖ hoarse
- Ⓗ haorse

17.
- Ⓐ wer
- Ⓑ war
- Ⓒ wur
- Ⓓ warr

3.
- Ⓐ toward
- Ⓑ towerd
- Ⓒ toword
- Ⓓ twoard

8.
- Ⓔ caugh
- Ⓕ cought
- Ⓖ cough
- Ⓗ cugh

13.
- Ⓐ form
- Ⓑ furm
- Ⓒ fom
- Ⓓ forrm

18.
- Ⓔ daghter
- Ⓕ dauhter
- Ⓖ daughter
- Ⓗ daugter

4.
- Ⓔ ofice
- Ⓕ office
- Ⓖ oficce
- Ⓗ afice

9.
- Ⓐ brougt
- Ⓑ brouht
- Ⓒ brooght
- Ⓓ brought

14.
- Ⓔ ror
- Ⓕ roar
- Ⓖ rore
- Ⓗ raor

19.
- Ⓐ jur
- Ⓑ jaw
- Ⓒ jer
- Ⓓ jaur

5.
- Ⓐ olready
- Ⓑ alredy
- Ⓒ already
- Ⓓ allready

10.
- Ⓔ ofer
- Ⓕ offer
- Ⓖ awfur
- Ⓗ ofur

15.
- Ⓐ corus
- Ⓑ choras
- Ⓒ chorus
- Ⓓ chorrus

20.
- Ⓔ awful
- Ⓕ awfull
- Ⓖ awfil
- Ⓗ auful

Words with /är/ and /âr/

Pretest Directions

Fold back the paper along the dotted line. Use the blanks to write each word as it is read aloud. When you finish the test, unfold the paper. Use the list at the right to correct any spelling mistakes. Practice the words you missed for the Posttest.

To Parents

Here are the results of your child's weekly spelling Pretest. You can help your child study for the Posttest by following these simple steps for each word on the word list:

1. Read the word to your child.

2. Have your child write the word, saying each letter as it is written.

3. Say each letter of the word as your child checks the spelling.

4. If a mistake has been made, have your child read each letter of the correctly spelled word aloud, and then repeat steps 1–3.

1. _____ 1. apart
2. _____ 2. hardly
3. _____ 3. yarn
4. _____ 4. army
5. _____ 5. marbles
6. _____ 6. repair
7. _____ 7. careful
8. _____ 8. scare
9. _____ 9. somewhere
10. _____ 10. wear
11. _____ 11. starve
12. _____ 12. barber
13. _____ 13. carnival
14. _____ 14. carpet
15. _____ 15. unfair
16. _____ 16. therefore
17. _____ 17. dairy
18. _____ 18. hare
19. _____ 19. prepare
20. _____ 20. pear

Challenge Words

_____ confusion

_____ hilltop

_____ lodge

_____ messenger

_____ praised

Words with /är/ and /âr/

Using the Word Study Steps

1. **LOOK** at the word.

2. **SAY** the word aloud.

3. **STUDY** the letters in the word.

4. **WRITE** the word.

5. **CHECK** the word.

   Did you spell the word right?
   If not, go back to step 1.

Spelling Tip

Look for word chunks or smaller words that help you remember the spelling of a word. For example:

somewhere =
some + where

Hide and Seek

Where are the spelling words hiding? Circle all the spelling words.

```
a a p a r t c c h a r d l y y a r n x a r m y
m a r b l e s v v r e p a i r c a w e a r z z
b z c a r e f u l n n s c a r e c c c a r p e t
s o m e w h e r e a a t h e r e f o r e x x
s t a r v e c a b a r b e r c a d a i r y a b
c a r n i v a l k k u n f a i r a a h a r e z z z
x a a p r e p a r e v v p e a r a a c c a
```

To Parents or Helpers

Using the Word Study Steps above as your child comes across any new words will help him or her learn to spell words effectively. Review the steps as you both go over this week's spelling words.

Go over the Spelling Tip with your child. Ask him or her to find helpful chunks or smaller words in other new words.

Help your child find and circle the spelling words in the puzzle.

Words with /är/ and /âr/

apart	marbles	somewhere	carnival	dairy
hardly	repair	wear	carpet	hare
yarn	careful	starve	unfair	prepare
army	scare	barber	therefore	pear

Sort each spelling word by finding the spelling pattern to which it belongs: /är/, spelled *ar*, or /âr/, spelled *air, are, ear,* or *ere*. Write the word and underline the spelling pattern letters.

Words with /är/ spelled

ar　　[b<u>ar</u>n]

1. _____
2. _____
3. _____
4. _____
5. _____
6. _____
7. _____
8. _____
9. _____

Words with /âr/ spelled

air　　[h<u>air</u>]

10. _____
11. _____
12. _____

Words with /âr/ spelled

are　　[p<u>are</u>]

13. _____
14. _____
15. _____
16. _____

ear　　[t<u>ear</u>]

17. _____
18. _____

ere　　[wh<u>ere</u>]

19. _____
20. _____

Words with /är/ and /âr/

apart	marbles	somewhere	carnival	dairy
hardly	repair	wear	carpet	hare
yarn	careful	starve	unfair	prepare
army	scare	barber	therefore	pear

Complete each sentence below with a spelling word listed above.

1. We watched the _____ march in the parade.

2. Please be _____ when you step off the bus.

3. Your lost mittens must be _____ in the playground.

4. Which outfit will you _____ to school today?

5. It is _____ to cut in front of another person in line.

6. I left my umbrella at home and, _____, got wet in the rain.

7. We went to the _____ to buy milk and cream.

8. I'll eat the apple, and you can eat the _____.

Similar Meanings
Write the spelling word that has the same, or almost the same, meaning .

9. hairdresser _____

10. separate _____

11. barely _____

12. string _____

13. fix _____

14. frighten _____

15. glass balls _____

16. hunger _____

17. festival _____

18. rug _____

19. rabbit _____

20. make _____

Words with /är/ and /âr/

Proofreading Activity

There are six spelling mistakes in this journal entry. Circle the misspelled spelling words. Write the words correctly on the lines below.

The Giant

There once was a giant. When he walked, the ground shook and made loud noises no matter how cairful he was. Thearfore, he prepaired a carepet made of soft yairn, and flew up to the sky. Today when you hear thunder, it is only the giant walking somewhear on the clouds.

1. _____ 3. _____ 5. _____

2. _____ 4. _____ 6. _____

Writing Activity

A legend is a story handed down through the years that many people believe, but that is not entirely true. Using four spelling words, write a make-believe legend that ends by explaining why something happens in nature, such as rain, lightning, snow, the sun or the moon.

_____

_____

_____

_____

Words with /är/ and /âr/

Look at the words in each set below. One word in each set is spelled correctly. Use a pencil to fill in the circle next to the correct word. Before you begin, look at the sample sets of words. Sample A has been done for you. Do Sample B by yourself. When you are sure you know what to do, you may go on with the rest of the page.

Sample A
- Ⓐ tairget
- Ⓑ target
- Ⓒ tareget
- Ⓓ tearget

Sample B
- Ⓔ whear
- Ⓕ where
- Ⓖ whair
- Ⓗ wher

1.
- Ⓐ barber
- Ⓑ berbar
- Ⓒ barbar
- Ⓓ airber

6.
- Ⓔ repare
- Ⓕ repere
- Ⓖ reper
- Ⓗ repair

11.
- Ⓐ stairve
- Ⓑ stareve
- Ⓒ stearve
- Ⓓ starve

16.
- Ⓔ heare
- Ⓕ hare
- Ⓖ haire
- Ⓗ harre

2.
- Ⓔ paer
- Ⓕ pere
- Ⓖ pear
- Ⓗ paire

7.
- Ⓐ carfull
- Ⓑ careful
- Ⓒ carefull
- Ⓓ cairful

12.
- Ⓔ waer
- Ⓕ wear
- Ⓖ wair
- Ⓗ weer

17.
- Ⓐ hairdly
- Ⓑ heardly
- Ⓒ hardly
- Ⓓ heredly

3.
- Ⓐ somwere
- Ⓑ somwhere
- Ⓒ somehere
- Ⓓ somewhere

8.
- Ⓔ dary
- Ⓕ darey
- Ⓖ deary
- Ⓗ dairy

13.
- Ⓐ mairbles
- Ⓑ marebles
- Ⓒ marbles
- Ⓓ mearbles

18.
- Ⓔ thearefore
- Ⓕ therefor
- Ⓖ thearfor
- Ⓗ therefore

4.
- Ⓔ prepair
- Ⓕ prepare
- Ⓖ prepere
- Ⓗ prepeer

9.
- Ⓐ carnival
- Ⓑ carnaval
- Ⓒ carnivail
- Ⓓ carnivale

14.
- Ⓔ scair
- Ⓕ scare
- Ⓖ scere
- Ⓗ scear

19.
- Ⓐ airmy
- Ⓑ army
- Ⓒ arme
- Ⓓ airme

5.
- Ⓐ unfair
- Ⓑ unfare
- Ⓒ unfiar
- Ⓓ unfar

10.
- Ⓔ cairpet
- Ⓕ carepet
- Ⓖ carpet
- Ⓗ cairpat

15.
- Ⓐ yarn
- Ⓑ yairn
- Ⓒ yaarn
- Ⓓ yarne

20.
- Ⓔ apairt
- Ⓕ apeart
- Ⓖ apart
- Ⓗ apatre

Words with /îr/ and /ûr/

Fold back the paper along the dotted line. Use the blanks to write each word as it is read aloud. When you finish the test, unfold the paper. Use the list at the right to correct any spelling mistakes. Practice the words you missed for the Posttest.

To Parents
Here are the results of your child's weekly spelling Pretest. You can help your child study for the Posttest by following these simple steps for each word on the word list:

1. Read the word to your child.

2. Have your child write the word, saying each letter as it is written.

3. Say each letter of the word as your child checks the spelling.

4. If a mistake has been made, have your child read each letter of the correctly spelled word aloud, then repeat steps 1–3.

1. _____
2. _____
3. _____
4. _____
5. _____
6. _____
7. _____
8. _____
9. _____
10. _____
11. _____
12. _____
13. _____
14. _____
15. _____
16. _____
17. _____
18. _____
19. _____
20. _____

1. fern
2. curve
3. worst
4. shirt
5. clear
6. mere
7. cheer
8. serious
9. germ
10. burst
11. worse
12. swirl
13. gear
14. sincerely
15. volunteer
16. period
17. insert
18. purpose
19. twirling
20. spear

Challenge Words

_____
_____
_____
_____
_____

connected
endangered
overcome
poisonous
sponge

Words with /îr/ and /ûr/

Using the Word Study Steps

1. LOOK at the word.

2. SAY the word aloud.

3. STUDY the letters in the word.

4. WRITE the word.

5. CHECK the word.

   Did you spell the word right?
   If not, go back to step 1.

> **Spelling Tip**
>
> Divide the word into syllables and spell one part at a time.
>
> vol un teer

Circle the Words

In each line there are two words that have the same spelling pattern. Circle the two that match and underline the spelling pattern in each.

1.	fern	germ	green
2.	ship	shirt	twirling
3.	clear	spear	spot
4.	sincerely	sink	mere
5.	cheer	volunteer	change
6.	park	serious	period
7.	burst	purpose	broke
8.	water	worst	worse
9.	gear	spear	spot
10.	sweep	swirl	twirling
11.	germ	inside	insert
12.	curve	purpose	carve

To Parents or Helpers

    Using the Word Study Steps above as your child comes across any new words will help him or her learn to spell words effectively. Review the steps as you both go over this week's spelling words.

    Go over the Spelling Tip with your child. Ask him or her to see which words on the list can be divided into syllables.

    Help your child cross out the words that do not match the patterns.

Words with /îr/ and /ûr/

fern	clear	germ	gear	insert
curve	mere	burst	sincerely	purpose
worst	cheer	worse	volunteer	twirling
shirt	serious	swirl	period	spear

Follow the Pattern

This week's words have the sounds /ûr/ and /îr/. Sort each spelling word by finding the sound and spelling pattern to which it belongs.

Write the spelling words for the sound /ûr/ spelled

ur

1. _____

2. _____

3. _____

er

4. _____

5. _____

6. _____

ir

7. _____

8. _____

9. _____

or

10. _____

11. _____

Write the spelling words that have /îr/ spelled

ear

12. _____

13. _____

14. _____

eer

15. _____

16. _____

ere

17. _____

18. _____

er

19. _____

20. _____

Words with /îr/ and /ûr/

fern	clear	germ	gear	insert
curve	mere	burst	sincerely	purpose
worst	cheer	worse	volunteer	twirling
shirt	serious	swirl	period	spear

Complete the Sentences

Complete each sentence with a spelling word or words.

1. The little girl laughed when her balloon _____.

2. Put a _____ at the end of a sentence.

3. In the forest, we found a leafy green _____ .

4. That is the _____ music I ever heard!

5. The flags twist and _____ in the wind.

6. The damage to the roof of the barn got _____ after the last storm.

7. A _____ is too small to see without a microscope.

8. I _____ hope you feel better soon.

Match Up

Write the spelling word that matches each meaning below.

9. equipment _____

10. circling _____

11. a little bit _____

12. offer help _____

13. a reason _____

14. pointed object _____

15. a garment _____

16. to put in _____

17. transparent _____

18. happiness _____

19. solemn _____

20. bend _____

Challenge Extension: Have students use the
Challenge Words to write an advertisement for a job as
112 an underwater explorer.

Grade 4/Unit 4
Meet an Underwater Explorer | 20

Words with /îr/ and /ûr/

Proofreading Activity

There are six spelling mistakes in this newspaper article. Circle the misspelled words. Write the words correctly on the lines below.

Twirling Fish Discovered!

Underwater explorer Syd Harris has discovered a new type of fish. He first saw it swimming in a swerl of water. Harris, a voluntere on this exploration, is very serous about preserving ocean life. "Not caring for the ocean would be the wurst thing that could happen," Harris said. "I sinceerely think that keeping the water clean and clear is a great perpose to have."

1. _____   3. _____   5. _____

2. _____   4. _____   6. _____

Writing Activity

Imagine that you are an underwater explorer. Write a page in a scrap book describing something new you found on your last trip. Use four spelling words.

_____

_____

_____

_____

Words with /îr/ and /ûr/

Look at the words in each set below. One word in each set is spelled correctly. Use a pencil to fill in the circle next to the correct word. Before you begin, look at the sample sets of words. Sample A has been done for you. Do Sample B by yourself. When you are sure you know what to do, you may go on with the rest of the page.

Sample A
(A) tairget   **Sample B**   (E) whear
(B) tareget   (F) where
(C) target   (G) whar
(D) tearget   (H) wher

1. (A) germ
   (B) girm
   (C) gurm
   (D) jerm

2. (E) berst
   (F) burst
   (G) birst
   (H) bers

3. (A) chear
   (B) chere
   (C) cher
   (D) cheer

4. (E) serious
   (F) sereous
   (G) searious
   (H) seerious

5. (A) wirse
   (B) worse
   (C) wurse
   (D) werse

6. (E) swerl
   (F) swurl
   (G) swirll
   (H) swirl

7. (A) speer
   (B) spere
   (C) spear
   (D) sper

8. (E) gear
   (F) geer
   (G) gere
   (H) ger

9. (A) twurling
   (B) twirling
   (C) twerling
   (D) twirlling

10. (E) cleer
    (F) clear
    (G) clere
    (H) cler

11. (A) sinceerly
    (B) sincearly
    (C) sincerly
    (D) sincerely

12. (E) volunteer
    (F) voluntear
    (G) voluntere
    (H) volunter

13. (A) mear
    (B) mere
    (C) meer
    (D) mer

14. (E) peeriod
    (F) peariod
    (G) period
    (H) pereiod

15. (A) shurt
    (B) shert
    (C) sherte
    (D) shirt

16. (E) pirpose
    (F) purrpose
    (G) purpose
    (H) perpose

17. (A) wirst
    (B) wourst
    (C) worst
    (D) werst

18. (E) insert
    (F) insurt
    (G) insirt
    (H) insort

19. (A) cerve
    (B) cirve
    (C) corve
    (D) curve

20. (E) fern
    (F) furn
    (G) firn
    (H) furnn

Compound Words

Fold back the paper along the dotted line. Use the blanks to write each word as it is read aloud. When you finish the test, unfold the paper. Use the list at the right to correct any spelling mistakes. Practice the words you missed for the Posttest.

To Parents
Here are the results of your child's weekly spelling Pretest. You can help your child study for the Posttest by following these simple steps for each word on the word list:

1. Read the word to your child.

2. Have your child write the word, saying each letter as it is written.

3. Say each letter of the word as your child checks the spelling.

4. If a mistake has been made, have your child read each letter of the correctly spelled word aloud, then repeat steps 1–3.

#		Word
1.	_____	1. bedroom
2.	_____	2. anymore
3.	_____	3. everybody
4.	_____	4. classroom
5.	_____	5. anyway
6.	_____	6. backyard
7.	_____	7. railroad
8.	_____	8. forever
9.	_____	9. bathtub
10.	_____	10. homemade
11.	_____	11. outline
12.	_____	12. windowpane
13.	_____	13. evergreens
14.	_____	14. grandparents
15.	_____	15. photocopy
16.	_____	16. whirlwinds
17.	_____	17. loudspeaker
18.	_____	18. northwest
19.	_____	19. thunderstorm
20.	_____	20. bedspread

Challenge Words

_____ abandon

_____ available

_____ original

_____ research

_____ traditional

Compound Words

Using the Word Study Steps

1. LOOK at the word.

2. SAY the word aloud.

3. STUDY the letters in the word.

4. WRITE the word.

5. CHECK the word.

   Did you spell the word right?
   If not, go back to step 1.

Spelling Tip

Remember not to add or take away letters when two smaller words are combined to make a compound word.

class + room = classroom

Bits and Pieces

Join the first word on the left with the second word on the right that completes each compound spelling word. Match the words in column 1–10 first, then do the same in 11–20.

1. for	_____	room	11. north	_____	west
2. class	_____	road	12. grand	_____	speaker
3. bed	_____	ever	13. out	_____	greens
4. home	_____	yard	14. bed	_____	line
5. bath	_____	more	15. thunder	_____	pane
6. any	_____	way	16. photo	_____	spread
7. every	_____	made	17. ever	_____	copy
8. any	_____	room	18. window	_____	storm
9. rail	_____	body	19. loud	_____	parents
10. back	_____	tub	20. whirl	_____	winds

To Parents or Helpers

   Using the Word Study Steps above as your child comes across any new words will help him or her learn to spell words effectively. Review the steps as you both go over this week's spelling words.
   Go over the Spelling Tip with your child. Ask your child to look at this week's spelling list to see that letters are not added or taken away from the two smaller words in each of the compound words.
   Help your child complete the spelling activity by matching the two words that make up each compound word.

Compound Words

bedroom	anyway	bathtub	evergreens	loudspeaker
anymore	backyard	homemade	grandparents	northwest
everybody	railroad	outline	photocopy	thunderstorm
classroom	forever	windowpane	whirlwinds	bedspread

Sort the spelling words according to number of syllables.

Two syllables

1. _____   6. _____

2. _____   7. _____

3. _____   8. _____

4. _____   9. _____

5. _____   10. _____

Three syllables

11. _____   15. _____

12. _____   16. _____

13. _____   17. _____

14. _____   18. _____

Four syllables

19. _____   20. _____

Compound Words

bedroom	anyway	bathtub	evergreens	loudspeaker
anymore	backyard	homemade	grandparents	northwest
everybody	railroad	outline	photocopy	thunderstorm
classroom	forever	windowpane	whirlwinds	bedspread

Meaning Match
Write the spelling word that matches each clue below.

1. If it's made at home it is _____.

2. You can take a bath in a _____.

3. A room where you sleep is a _____.

4. Always means _____.

5. A place where you learn is a _____.

6. A noisy storm is a _____.

7. Trees that never lose their leaves are _____.

8. A plan for writing is an _____.

9. Your parents' parents are your _____.

10 Glass in a window is the _____.

11. The comforter on a bed is a _____.

12. One kind of copy is a _____.

13. My hat was swept off my head by _____.

14. The direction toward the next town is _____.

15. Sound can be made louder by using a _____.

Challenge Extension: Have the students write sentences using blanks for each Challenge Word. Have them trade papers with a partner and fill each other's missing words.

Compound Words

Proofreading Activity

There are six spelling mistakes in this flyer. Circle the misspelled words. Write the words correctly on the lines below.

Everbody can find information to write a report!
1. First, look up your subject, such as everrgreens, grandparents, or whirwinds.
2. Then make a photcopy of the articles you find on the subject. (You can read the photocopies at home in your bedroom or even in the battub!)
3. Finally, take the photocopies to your classroom and make an outine.
Now you are ready to write!

1. _____   3. _____   5. _____

2. _____   4. _____   6. _____

Writing Activity

Write some questions you would like to ask Joanna Cole about her career using four spelling words.

_____

_____

_____

_____

Compound Words

Look at the words in each set below. One word in each set is spelled correctly. Use a pencil to fill in the circle next to the correct word. Before you begin, look at the sample sets of words. Sample A has been done for you. Do Sample B by yourself. When you are sure you know what to do, you may go on with the rest of the page.

Sample A
- Ⓐ fotball
- Ⓑ futball
- Ⓒ foottball
- ● football

Sample B
- Ⓔ bacbone
- Ⓕ backbone
- Ⓖ bakbone
- Ⓗ backbon

1.
- Ⓐ bedsspread
- Ⓑ beddspread
- Ⓒ bedspread
- Ⓓ bedspred

2.
- Ⓔ grandparents
- Ⓕ granparents
- Ⓖ grannparents
- Ⓗ grandparints

3.
- Ⓐ evergeens
- Ⓑ evergreins
- Ⓒ evergrens
- Ⓓ evergreens

4.
- Ⓔ photcopy
- Ⓕ photocopy
- Ⓖ photocupy
- Ⓗ photocopie

5.
- Ⓐ loudpeaker
- Ⓑ loudspeeker
- Ⓒ loudspeaker
- Ⓓ lowdspeaker

6.
- Ⓔ northwest
- Ⓕ nortwest
- Ⓖ northhwest
- Ⓗ nortwesth

7.
- Ⓐ thonderstorm
- Ⓑ thunderstorm
- Ⓒ thundersorm
- Ⓓ thunterstorm

8.
- Ⓔ homemad
- Ⓕ homemaid
- Ⓖ hommade
- Ⓗ homemade

9.
- Ⓐ outline
- Ⓑ outeline
- Ⓒ outlline
- Ⓓ owtline

10.
- Ⓔ windowpan
- Ⓕ windowpane
- Ⓖ windowpain
- Ⓗ windopane

11.
- Ⓐ everbody
- Ⓑ everybodey
- Ⓒ everyody
- Ⓓ everybody

12.
- Ⓔ raillroad
- Ⓕ railrroad
- Ⓖ railroad
- Ⓗ raleroad

13.
- Ⓐ bakyard
- Ⓑ backyard
- Ⓒ backard
- Ⓓ bacyard

14.
- Ⓔ forever
- Ⓕ forver
- Ⓖ forrever
- Ⓗ forevur

15.
- Ⓐ anyore
- Ⓑ enymore
- Ⓒ anymore
- Ⓓ annymore

16.
- Ⓔ battub
- Ⓕ bathtub
- Ⓖ bathub
- Ⓗ bathttub

17.
- Ⓐ whirlinds
- Ⓑ whirwinds
- Ⓒ whirlwinds
- Ⓓ whirllwinds

18.
- Ⓔ clasroom
- Ⓕ classroom
- Ⓖ classrroom
- Ⓗ classrom

19.
- Ⓐ anyay
- Ⓑ anway
- Ⓒ anyway
- Ⓓ anywey

20.
- Ⓔ bedroom
- Ⓕ beddroom
- Ⓖ bedrroom
- Ⓗ bedrom

Words from Science

Fold back the paper along the dotted line. Use the blanks to write each word as it is read aloud. When you finish the test, unfold the paper. Use the list at the right to correct any spelling mistakes. Practice the words you missed for the Posttest.

To Parents
Here are the results of your child's weekly spelling Pretest. You can help your child study for the Posttest by following these simple steps for each word on the word list:

1. Read the word to your child.

2. Have your child write the word, saying each letter as it is written.

3. Say each letter of the word as your child checks the spelling.

4. If a mistake has been made, have your child read each letter of the correctly spelled word aloud, then repeat steps 1–3.

#		Word
1.	_____	1. shells
2.	_____	2. crabs
3.	_____	3. liquid
4.	_____	4. fact
5.	_____	5. butterfly
6.	_____	6. discovered
7.	_____	7. cast
8.	_____	8. lobster
9.	_____	9. hatch
10.	_____	10. expert
11.	_____	11. mineral
12.	_____	12. dolphin
13.	_____	13. systems
14.	_____	14. clam
15.	_____	15. imprint
16.	_____	16. kelp
17.	_____	17. caterpillar
18.	_____	18. depth
19.	_____	19. skeleton
20.	_____	20. fungus

Challenge Words

_____ ancestors
_____ disaster
_____ microscope
_____ snout
_____ weird

Words from Science

Using the Word Study Steps

1. LOOK at the word.

2. SAY the word aloud.

3. STUDY the letters in the word.

4. WRITE the word.

5. CHECK the word.

Did you spell the word right?
If not, go back to step 1.

Spelling Tip

Think of times you may have seen the word while reading, or on signs, or in your textbook. Try to remember how the word looked. Write the word by spelling it different ways. Which one looks correct?

~~dolfin~~, ~~dolpin~~, dolphin

Hide and Seek

Where are the spelling words hiding? Circle all the spelling words.

xymineralaacaterpillarvxcastaliquidbbsystemsxx

factaaakelpxxsdiscoveredxyabhatchxvexpertxiv

xxlobsterabdolphinvvximprintxxfungusaabcrabsx

xvvbutterflyaaclamxvvdepthxxshellsyaaskeleton

To Parents or Helpers:

Using the Word Study Steps above as your child comes across any new words will help him or her learn to spell words effectively. Review the steps as you both go over this week's spelling words.

Go over the Spelling Tip with your child. Help your child write a word different ways to see which one looks correct.

Help your child complete the spelling activity.

Words from Science

shells	butterfly	hatch	systems	caterpillar
crabs	discovered	expert	clam	depth
liquid	cast	mineral	imprint	skeleton
fact	lobster	dolphin	kelp	fungus

Write the spelling words under the correct spelling pattern.

a

1. _____   4. _____

2. _____   5. _____

3. _____   6. _____

e   *i*

7. _____   12. _____

8. _____   13. _____

9. _____   14. _____

10. _____   15. _____

11. _____   16. _____

o   *u*

17. _____   19. _____

18. _____   20. _____

Words from Science

shells	butterfly	hatch	systems	caterpillar
crabs	discovered	expert	clam	depth
liquid	cast	mineral	imprint	skeleton
fact	lobster	dolphin	kelp	fungus

Complete each sentence with a spelling word.

1. Is that a _____ or an opinion?

2. _____ is a kind of seaweed.

3. Our feet left an _____ in the wet sand.

4. A _____ is hidden inside its two shells.

5. A mushroom is a type of _____.

6. Look at the fuzzy _____ inching up the leaf!

7. When water freezes, it becomes a solid rather than a _____.

8. The chicks will _____ from the eggs today.

9. There are many bones in the human _____.

10. The red _____ has two big front claws.

11. We can swim to a _____ of 15 feet.

12. The _____ scurry across the sand.

13. I have a plaster _____ on my broken leg.

14. If it's not plant or animal, it must be _____.

15. We made a necklace from the _____ we found on the beach.

Challenge Extension: Students can create sentences with each
Challenge word, but leave out the word. Then have students exchange
papers to see if they can complete each other's sentences by adding
the missing Challenge word.

Words from Science

Proofreading Activity

There are six spelling mistakes in this lab report. Circle the misspelled words. Write the words correctly on the lines below.

Today in the lab we examined a clam, a lobstur , a butturfly, and a caterpillar to see how each of their sytems works. We also saw the skelaton of a dolfin as well as a few shells and some kelp.

1. _____   3. _____   5. _____

2. _____   4. _____   6. _____

Writing Activity

Imagine you could go back in time, about 500 million years ago. Write a news broadcast describing the animals you see all around you. Use four spelling words.

_____

_____

_____

_____

Words from Science

Look at the words in each set below. One word in each set is spelled correctly. Use a pencil to fill in the circle next to the correct word. Before you begin, look at the sample sets of words. Sample A has been done for you. Do Sample B by yourself. When you are sure you know what to do, you may go on with the rest of the page.

Sample A
- (A) bady
- (B) bahdy
- (C) body
- (D) boddy

Sample B
- (E) mach
- (F) mattch
- (G) match
- (H) metch

1.
- (A) hatch
- (B) hetch
- (C) haitch
- (D) hotch

6.
- (E) expart
- (F) expurt
- (G) expert
- (H) expirt

11.
- (A) discovered
- (B) dascovered
- (C) descovered
- (D) duscovered

16.
- (E) fict
- (F) fect
- (G) fact
- (H) fack

2.
- (E) dalphin
- (F) dolphin
- (G) delphin
- (H) dolfin

7.
- (A) imprint
- (B) imprit
- (C) imprent
- (D) impront

12.
- (E) dapth
- (F) depth
- (G) dipth
- (H) dupth

17.
- (A) caterpillar
- (B) coterpillar
- (C) ceterpillar
- (D) caterpillur

3.
- (A) labster
- (B) lebster
- (C) lubster
- (D) lobster

8.
- (E) clem
- (F) clam
- (G) clim
- (H) clamm

13.
- (A) batterfly
- (B) betterfly
- (C) butterfly
- (D) botterfly

18.
- (E) kilp
- (F) kelp
- (G) kulp
- (H) kalp

4.
- (E) maneral
- (F) meneral
- (G) muneral
- (H) mineral

9.
- (A) fungos
- (B) fungis
- (C) fungas
- (D) fungus

14.
- (E) kast
- (F) cest
- (G) cust
- (H) cast

19.
- (A) craibs
- (B) crubs
- (C) crabs
- (D) crebs

5.
- (A) sistems
- (B) systtems
- (C) systems
- (D) sestems

10.
- (E) skaleton
- (F) skeleton
- (G) skelaton
- (H) skeliton

15.
- (A) liquod
- (B) liqued
- (C) liqud
- (D) liquid

20.
- (E) shalls
- (F) shaills
- (G) shulls
- (H) shells

Grade 4/Unit 4 Review Test

Read each sentence. If an underlined word is spelled wrong, fill in the circle that goes with that word. If no word is spelled wrong, fill in the circle below NONE. Read Sample A, and do Sample B.

A. His <u>dawter</u> had <u>already</u> driven the <u>car</u>.
     A   B   C

NONE
A. Ⓐ Ⓑ Ⓒ Ⓓ

B. An <u>army</u> of ants walked <u>toward</u> the <u>fern</u>.
     E   F   G

NONE
B. Ⓔ Ⓕ Ⓖ Ⓗ

1. The <u>auther</u> used a writing <u>form</u> that would <u>scare</u> the reader.
     A   B   C

NONE
1. Ⓐ Ⓑ Ⓒ Ⓓ

2. A <u>volunteer</u> will arrive at the <u>dairry</u> by <u>dawn</u>.
     E   F   G

NONE
2. Ⓔ Ⓕ Ⓖ Ⓗ

3. The <u>serious</u> illness gave him a <u>hoarse</u> <u>caugh</u>.
     A   B   C

NONE
3. Ⓐ Ⓑ Ⓒ Ⓓ

4. The <u>barbar</u>, <u>twirling</u> his mustache, looked <u>serious</u>.
     E   F   G

NONE
4. Ⓔ Ⓕ Ⓖ Ⓗ

5. The <u>pear</u> trees and <u>evergreens</u> seem to go on <u>forrever</u>.
     A   B   C

NONE
5. Ⓐ Ⓑ Ⓒ Ⓓ

6. The <u>bedspread</u> was dusty and <u>therefor</u> made him <u>cough</u>.
     E   F   G

NONE
6. Ⓔ Ⓕ Ⓖ Ⓗ

7. The <u>lobster</u> could <u>speer</u> the <u>pear</u> with his claw.
     A   B   C

NONE
7. Ⓐ Ⓑ Ⓒ Ⓓ

8. A dangerous <u>germ</u> caused a <u>scair</u> at the <u>dairy</u>.
              E   F   G

NONE
8. Ⓔ Ⓕ Ⓖ Ⓗ

9. The <u>whirlwinds</u> caused a <u>scare</u> at the <u>barber</u> shop.
     A   B   C

NONE
9. Ⓐ Ⓑ Ⓒ Ⓓ

10. There's a <u>photocopy</u> of <u>kelp</u> and <u>evergreens</u>.
           E   F   G

NONE
10. Ⓔ Ⓕ Ⓖ Ⓗ

11. The <u>catterpillar</u> will change its <u>form</u> to a <u>butterfly</u>.
     A   B   C

NONE
11. Ⓐ Ⓑ Ⓒ Ⓓ

Grade 4 Unit 4 Review Test

12. At <u>dawn</u> we saw a <u>lobstir</u> covered in <u>kelp</u>.
    E   F   G

12. Ⓔ Ⓕ Ⓖ Ⓗ NONE

13. The <u>whirlwinds</u> sent the <u>bedspread</u> <u>twirrling</u> away.
     A   B   C

13. Ⓐ Ⓑ Ⓒ Ⓓ NONE

14. It seems like the <u>lobster</u> swims in <u>likwid</u> <u>forever</u>.
             E   F   G

14. Ⓔ Ⓕ Ⓖ Ⓗ NONE

15. "<u>Therefore</u>, I made a <u>photocopy</u>," said the <u>author</u>.
     A   B   C

15. Ⓐ Ⓑ Ⓒ Ⓓ NONE

16. The <u>voluntier</u> was <u>hoarse</u> from a <u>serious</u> cold.
    E   F   G

16. Ⓔ Ⓕ Ⓖ Ⓗ NONE

17. The <u>caterpillar</u> ate <u>kelp</u> before changing to a <u>butterflie</u>.
     A   B   C

17. Ⓐ Ⓑ Ⓒ Ⓓ NONE

18. The <u>liquid</u> soap at the <u>barber</u> shop can kill any <u>germ</u>.
    E   F   G

18. Ⓔ Ⓕ Ⓖ Ⓗ NONE

19. I will <u>volunteer</u> to <u>photokopy</u> a picture of this <u>caterpillar</u>.
        A   B   C

19. Ⓐ Ⓑ Ⓒ Ⓓ NONE

20. If you drink a <u>liquid</u>, it may help your <u>hoars</u> <u>cough</u>.
           E   F G

20. Ⓔ Ⓕ Ⓖ Ⓗ NONE

21. The <u>spear</u> had the <u>forme</u> of a <u>butterfly</u> on its handle.
     A   B   C

21. Ⓐ Ⓑ Ⓒ Ⓓ NONE

22. The <u>author</u> woke up at <u>dawn</u> and ate a <u>pear</u>.
    E   F   G

22. Ⓔ Ⓕ Ⓖ Ⓗ NONE

23. The <u>twirling</u> <u>wirlwinds</u> went through me like a <u>spear</u>.
     A   B   C

23. Ⓐ Ⓑ Ⓒ Ⓓ NONE

24. Sewing the <u>evergreens</u> on the <u>bedspred</u> took <u>forever</u>.
        E   F   G

24. Ⓔ Ⓕ Ⓖ Ⓗ NONE

25. A <u>girm</u> got in the milk; <u>therefore</u> the <u>dairy</u> closed.
    A   B   C

25. Ⓐ Ⓑ Ⓒ Ⓓ NONE

Words with /s/ and /f/

Pretest Directions

Fold back the paper along the dotted line. Use the blanks to write each word as it is read aloud. When you finish the test, unfold the paper. Use the list at the right to correct any spelling mistakes. Practice the words you missed for the Posttest.

To Parents

Here are the results of your child's weekly spelling Pretest. You can help your child study for the Posttest by following these simple steps for each word on the word list:

1. Read the word to your child.

2. Have your child write the word, saying each letter as it is written.

3. Say each letter of the word as your child checks the spelling.

4. If a mistake has been made, have your child read each letter of the correctly spelled word aloud, and then repeat steps 1–3.

1. _____	1. mess
2. _____	2. sorry
3. _____	3. balance
4. _____	4. police
5. _____	5. classic
6. _____	6. rough
7. _____	7. certain
8. _____	8. telephone
9. _____	9. surprise
10. _____	10. elephant
11. _____	11. laughter
12. _____	12. citizen
13. _____	13. advice
14. _____	14. photograph
15. _____	15. cider
16. _____	16. alphabet
17. _____	17. triumph
18. _____	18. careless
19. _____	19. tough
20. _____	20. enormous

Challenge Words

_____ amazement

_____ destroyed

_____ eldest

_____ fowl

_____ strewn

Words with /s/ and /f/

Using the Word Study Steps

1. LOOK at the word.

2. SAY the word aloud.

3. STUDY the letters in the word.

4. WRITE the word.

5. CHECK the word.

   Did you spell the word right?
   If not, go back to step 1.

Spelling Tip

When the /s/ sound is spelled *c*, *c* is always followed by *e*, *i*, or *y*. For example:

certain   cider   fancy

Word Scramble

Unscramble each set of letters to make a spelling word.

1. celnaab _____

2. esspriur _____

3. irdce _____

4. grooappthh _____

5. znetiic _____

6. phmtiur _____

7. museoorn _____

8. hgrou _____

9. ugtho _____

10. acevid _____

11. ssliacc _____

12. tneephole _____

13. sesm _____

14. aerhtgul _____

15. rtaince _____

16. taepbhal _____

17. alreessc _____

18. eeantlhp _____

19. ryrso _____

20. lceipo _____

To Parents or Helpers

Using the Word Study Steps above as your child comes across any new words will help him or her learn to spell words effectively. Review the steps as you both go over this week's spelling words.

Go over the Spelling Tip with your child. Ask your child to find other spelling words in which *c* has the /s/ sound and is followed by *e*, *i* or *y*.

Help your child complete the spelling activity.

Words with /s/ and /f/

mess	classic	surprise	advice	triumph
sorry	rough	elephant	photograph	careless
balance	certain	laughter	cider	tough
police	telephone	citizen	alphabet	enormous

Sort each spelling word by finding the spelling pattern to which it belongs. Write the word and circle the spelling pattern letter or letters.

Write the spelling words that have /s/ spelled:

ss

1. _____

2. _____

3. _____

s

4. _____

5. _____

6. _____

c

7. _____

8. _____

9. _____

ce

10. _____

11. _____

12. _____

Write the spelling words that have /f/ spelled:

ph

13. _____

14. _____

15. _____

16. _____

17. _____

gh

18. _____

19. _____

20. _____

Words with /s/ and /f/

mess	classic	surprise	advice	triumph
sorry	rough	elephant	photograph	careless
balance	certain	laughter	cider	tough
police	telephone	citizen	alphabet	enormous

Synonym Alert!

Write the spelling words that have the same meaning as the words below.

1. sympathetic _____

2. sure _____

3. law officers _____

4. suggestion _____

5. snapshot _____

6. victory _____

7. strong _____

8. shock _____

9. reckless _____

10. resident _____

Sentence Sense

Complete each sentence with the spelling word that fits the context.

11. What a _____ the dog made tracking in mud!

12. The _____ has a very loud ring.

13. Sandpaper feels very _____ and scratchy.

14. We saw a big gray _____ at the circus.

15. The huge elephant was _____!

16. There are 26 letters in the _____.

17. Would you like another glass of apple _____?

18. It's hard to keep your _____ when walking on stilts!

132

Challenge Extension: Invite students to make a crossword puzzle using the Challenge Words.

Grade 4/Unit 5
The Fox and the Guinea Pig 18

Words with /s/ and /f/

Proofreading Activity

There are six spelling mistakes in this paragraph. Circle the misspelled words.
Write the words correctly on the lines below.

It's tuff being a fox! I'm sory that I ever met a guinea pig. What a mess he got me
into! Maybe I was a little careles, but how was I to know I'd have such a ruff time?
It was a real surprize to me. I wish I'd met an elephant instead of a guinea pig.
Follow my advise and stay away from guinea pigs!

1. _____ 3. _____ 5. _____

2. _____ 4. _____ 6. _____

Writing Activity

Do you have any pets? If not, is there a pet you would like to have? Write a
paragraph about a pet you have or a pet you wish you had. Use at least four
spelling words.

_____

_____

_____

_____

Words with /s/ and /f/

Look at the words in each set below. One word in each set is spelled correctly. Use a pencil to fill in the circle next to the correct word. Before you begin, look at the sample sets of words. Sample A has been done for you. Do Sample B by yourself. When you are sure you know what to do, you may go on with the rest of the page.

Sample A
Ⓐ chanc
Ⓑ chanss
Ⓒ chans
Ⓓ chance ●

Sample B
Ⓔ graf
Ⓕ graff
Ⓖ graef
Ⓗ graph

1. Ⓐ alfabet
   Ⓑ alphabet
   Ⓒ alphebet
   Ⓓ alfebet

6. Ⓔ triumf
   Ⓕ trimpf
   Ⓖ triamph
   Ⓗ triumph

11. Ⓐ mes
    Ⓑ mecs
    Ⓒ messe
    Ⓓ mess

16. Ⓔ balance
    Ⓕ balans
    Ⓖ balence
    Ⓗ ballance

2. Ⓔ touf
   Ⓕ tuff
   Ⓖ tough
   Ⓗ toff

7. Ⓐ elefant
   Ⓑ elafant
   Ⓒ elephant
   Ⓓ elaphant

12. Ⓔ clasic
    Ⓕ classicc
    Ⓖ classic
    Ⓗ claasic

17. Ⓐ advice
    Ⓑ advies
    Ⓒ advisse
    Ⓓ advicce

3. Ⓐ careles
   Ⓑ carreles
   Ⓒ carelles
   Ⓓ careless

8. Ⓔ sitizen
   Ⓕ citizen
   Ⓖ sitisen
   Ⓗ citisen

13. Ⓐ polise
    Ⓑ police
    Ⓒ polis
    Ⓓ polace

18. Ⓔ photograf
    Ⓕ photograff
    Ⓖ photograph
    Ⓗ fotograph

4. Ⓔ enormouss
   Ⓕ enormous
   Ⓖ enorrmous
   Ⓗ enarmous

9. Ⓐ rouf
   Ⓑ raugh
   Ⓒ rough
   Ⓓ rouff

14. Ⓔ laughter
    Ⓕ lauffter
    Ⓖ laufter
    Ⓗ laghter

19. Ⓐ sider
    Ⓑ sidar
    Ⓒ cidar
    Ⓓ cider

5. Ⓐ telaphone
   Ⓑ telefon
   Ⓒ telefone
   Ⓓ telephone

10. Ⓔ certain
    Ⓕ sertain
    Ⓖ certin
    Ⓗ sertan

15. Ⓐ suprise
    Ⓑ surprisse
    Ⓒ surpise
    Ⓓ surprise

20. Ⓔ sory
    Ⓕ sorry
    Ⓖ sorie
    Ⓗ sorrie

Words with /ər/ and /chər/

Pretest Directions

Fold back the paper along the dotted line. Use the blanks to write each word as it is read aloud. When you finish the test, unfold the paper. Use the list at the right to correct any spelling mistakes. Practice the words you missed for the Posttest.

To Parents

Here are the results of your child's weekly spelling Pretest. You can help your child study for the Posttest by following these simple steps for each word on the word list:

1. Read the word to your child.

2. Have your child write the word, saying each letter as it is written.

3. Say each letter of the word as your child checks the spelling.

4. If a mistake has been made, have your child read each letter of the correctly spelled word aloud, then repeat steps 1–3.

1. _____	1. brother
2. _____	2. honor
3. _____	3. either
4. _____	4. popular
5. _____	5. number
6. _____	6. pictures
7. _____	7. odor
8. _____	8. enter
9. _____	9. vinegar
10. _____	10. capture
11. _____	11. member
12. _____	12. nature
13. _____	13. tender
14. _____	14. visitor
15. _____	15. polar
16. _____	16. anchor
17. _____	17. pasture
18. _____	18. chapter
19. _____	19. suffer
20. _____	20. furniture

Challenge Words

_____ errands

_____ instinct

_____ memorizing

_____ relieved

_____ sirens

Words with /ər/ and /chər/

Using the Word Study Steps

1. LOOK at the word.

2. SAY the word aloud.

3. STUDY the letters in the word.

4. WRITE the word.

5. CHECK the word.

   Did you spell the word right?
   If not, go back to step 1.

Spelling Tip

Become familiar with the dictionary and use it often.

Word Find

The spelling words are hiding in this puzzle. See if you can find and circle all 20 words.

```
picturesqcapturebodorabrotherzhonor
xeitherqxvinegaratenderbnatureaanchor
pasturebchapterxsufferbfurnitureapopular
numberaenterzimemberzzvisitorapolar
```

To Parents or Helpers

Using the Word Study Steps above as your child comes across any new words will help him or her learn to spell words effectively. Review the steps as you both go over this week's spelling words.

Go over the Spelling Tip with your child. Help your child look up spelling words in a dictionary.

Help your child complete the spelling activity.

Words with /ər/ and /chər/

brother	number	vinegar	tender	pasture
honor	pictures	capture	visitor	chapter
either	odor	member	polar	suffer
popular	enter	nature	anchor	furniture

End Game

This week's spelling words contain /ər/ and /chər/. Write each spelling word under the matching spelling.

/ər/ spelled

er

1. _____   5. _____

2. _____   6. _____

3. _____   7. _____

4. _____   8. _____

or   *ar*

9. _____   13. _____

10. _____   14. _____

11. _____   15. _____

12. _____

/chər/ spelled

ture

16. _____

17. _____

18. _____

19. _____

20. _____

Words with /ər/ and /chər/

brother	number	vinegar	tender	pasture
honor	pictures	capture	visitor	chapter
either	odor	member	polar	suffer
popular	enter	nature	anchor	furniture

Analogies

An analogy is a statement that compares sets of words that are alike in some way: **shoe** is to **foot** as **glove** is to **hand**. The analogy points out that your **foot** fits in your **shoe** the same as your **hand** fits in your **glove**.

Use spelling words to complete the analogies below.

1. **Dog** is to **poodle** as **bear** is to _____.

2. **Words** are to **stories** as **colors** are to _____.

3. **Sheep** are to **meadow** as **cows** are to _____.

4. **Girl** is to **sister** as **boy** is to _____.

5. **Writing** is to **letter** as **math** is to _____.

6. **Bread** is to **butter** as **salad** is to _____.

7. **Disliked** is to **rejected** as **favorite** is to _____.

8. **Home** is to **house** as **guest** is to _____.

9. **Whole** is to **part** as **book** is to _____.

10. **Shirt** is to **clothing** as **chair** is to _____.

Find the Opposites

Write the spelling word that is the opposite of each word.

11. disgrace _____   16. tough _____

12. neither _____   17. let go _____

13. enjoy _____   18. outcast _____

14. odorless _____   19. artificial _____

15. leave _____   20. sail _____

Challenge Extension: Ask students to write a synonym for each of the Challenge Words. Students can exchange papers with a friend to check their work.

138

Grade 4/Unit 5
Mom's Best Friend
20

Words with /ər/ and /chər/

Proofreading Activity

There are six spelling mistakes in this want ad. Circle the misspelled words. Write the words correctly on the lines below.

Wanted: Families to help train guide dogs. Every membur must be tendor and kind to animals. You will have to train the puppy to stay off the furnishure. Dogs shouldn't be scared of a visiter either. They must learn to deal with creatures in nasure, not to capsure them. It is an honor to help train a guide dog.

1. _____   3. _____   5. _____

2. _____   4. _____   6. _____

Writing Activity

Animals can help people in many different ways. Guide dogs can help lead blind people. Describe some ways that animals make life easier for people. Use four spelling words.

_____

_____

_____

_____

Words with /ər/ and /chər/

Look at the words in each set below. One word in each set is spelled correctly. Use a pencil to fill in the circle next to the correct word. Before you begin, look at the sample sets of words. Sample A has been done for you. Do Sample B by yourself. When you are sure you know what to do, you may go on with the rest of the page.

Sample A
- Ⓐ tertle
- Ⓑ tirtle
- Ⓒ turttle
- ● turtle

Sample B
- Ⓔ world
- Ⓕ wurld
- Ⓖ wirld
- Ⓗ werld

1.
- Ⓐ suffer
- Ⓑ suffar
- Ⓒ suffur
- Ⓓ suffor

6.
- Ⓔ passture
- Ⓕ pasture
- Ⓖ paschure
- Ⓗ pascure

11.
- Ⓐ capture
- Ⓑ capchure
- Ⓒ capsure
- Ⓓ capshure

16.
- Ⓔ vineger
- Ⓕ vinegor
- Ⓖ vinegar
- Ⓗ vinegur

2.
- Ⓔ chaptar
- Ⓕ chaptur
- Ⓖ chapter
- Ⓗ chaptor

7.
- Ⓐ visitor
- Ⓑ visiter
- Ⓒ visitar
- Ⓓ visitur

12.
- Ⓔ entur
- Ⓕ entar
- Ⓖ entor
- Ⓗ enter

17.
- Ⓐ popular
- Ⓑ populur
- Ⓒ populer
- Ⓓ populor

3.
- Ⓐ polar
- Ⓑ polur
- Ⓒ polor
- Ⓓ poler

8.
- Ⓔ tendor
- Ⓕ tendur
- Ⓖ tender
- Ⓗ tendar

13.
- Ⓐ odur
- Ⓑ oder
- Ⓒ odor
- Ⓓ odar

18.
- Ⓔ eithar
- Ⓕ eithor
- Ⓖ eithur
- Ⓗ either

4.
- Ⓔ anchar
- Ⓕ anchur
- Ⓖ ancher
- Ⓗ anchor

9.
- Ⓐ nature
- Ⓑ nachure
- Ⓒ nasure
- Ⓓ nasture

14.
- Ⓔ pictures
- Ⓕ picshures
- Ⓖ picsures
- Ⓗ piksures

19.
- Ⓐ honur
- Ⓑ honar
- Ⓒ honor
- Ⓓ honer

5.
- Ⓐ furnishure
- Ⓑ furnisure
- Ⓒ furniture
- Ⓓ furniscure

10.
- Ⓔ membar
- Ⓕ membur
- Ⓖ member
- Ⓗ membor

15.
- Ⓐ numbur
- Ⓑ number
- Ⓒ numbor
- Ⓓ numbar

20.
- Ⓔ brothor
- Ⓕ brothur
- Ⓖ brothar
- Ⓗ brother

Words with /əl/ and /ən/

Fold back the paper along the dotted line. Use the blanks to write each word as it is read aloud. When you finish the test, unfold the paper. Use the list at the right to correct any spelling mistakes. Practice the words you missed for the Posttest.

To Parents

Here are the results of your child's weekly spelling Pretest. You can help your child study for the Posttest by following these simple steps for each word on the word list:

1. Read the word to your child.

2. Have your child write the word, saying each letter as it is written.

3. Say each letter of the word as your child checks the spelling.

4. If a mistake has been made, have your child read each letter of the correctly spelled word aloud, then repeat steps 1–3.

1. _____	1. final
2. _____	2. uncle
3. _____	3. several
4. _____	4. model
5. _____	5. terrible
6. _____	6. pencil
7. _____	7. lion
8. _____	8. taken
9. _____	9. simple
10. _____	10. women
11. _____	11. reason
12. _____	12. gentle
13. _____	13. total
14. _____	14. settle
15. _____	15. level
16. _____	16. medical
17. _____	17. evil
18. _____	18. listen
19. _____	19. common
20. _____	20. cotton

Challenge Words

_____ attendants

_____ awkwardly

_____ celebration

_____ knowledge

_____ released

Words with /əl/ and /ən/

Using the Word Study Steps

1. LOOK at the word.

2. SAY the word aloud.

3. STUDY the letters in the word.

4. WRITE the word.

5. CHECK the word.

   Did you spell the word right?
   If not, go back to step 1.

Spelling Tip

Think of times you have read a word in a book, on a sign, or on a billboard. Try to remember how it looked. Then write the word in different ways. Which one looks correct?

finil   finul   final

| le | al | el | il | en | on |

End of the Line

Find the word ending from the box above that completes each spelling word below.

1. comm _____

2. list _____

3. fin _____

4. cott _____

5. unc _____

6. terrib _____

7. mod _____

8. li _____

9. reas _____

10. penc _____

11. tot _____

12. gent _____

13. lev _____

14. simp _____

15. sett _____

16. wom _____

17. ev _____

18. medic _____

19. tak _____

20. sever _____

To Parents or Helpers

Using the Word Study Steps above as your child comes across any new words will help him or her learn to spell words effectively. Review the steps as you both go over this week's spelling words.

Go over the Spelling Tip with your child. Help your child write some of the spelling words in different ways to figure out which one looks correct.

Help your child complete the spelling activity.

Words with /əl/ and /ən/

final	terrible	simple	total	evil
uncle	pencil	women	settle	listen
several	lion	reason	level	common
model	taken	gentle	medical	cotton

End Game

This week's spelling words contain /əl/ and /ən/. Write each spelling word under the correct spelling pattern ending.

/əl/ spelled

le

1. _____
2. _____
3. _____
4. _____
5. _____

al

6. _____
7. _____
8. _____
9. _____

el

10. _____
11. _____

il

12. _____
13. _____

/ən/ spelled

en

14. _____
15. _____
16. _____

on

17. _____
18. _____
19. _____
20. _____

Words with /əl/ and /ən/

final	terrible	simple	total	evil
uncle	pencil	women	settle	listen
several	lion	reason	level	common
model	taken	gentle	medical	cotton

Make Meanings

Write the spelling word that matches each clue below.

1. to add up _____

2. doctors and health _____

3. more than one woman _____

4. hear _____

5. king of the jungle _____

6. even _____

7. type of fabric _____

8. very bad _____

9. not hard _____

10. really awful _____

11. nice and kind _____

12. ordinary _____

13. more than two _____

14. tool used for writing _____

15. your aunt's husband _____

Sentence Sense

Fill in the correct spelling word in each sentence.

16. Have you already _____ your turn?

17. This is the _____ time you will get the chance to do better.

18. What _____ did she give for coming late to class?

19. A globe is a _____ of our world.

20. We should _____ our disagreement before we go home.

Challenge Extension: Invite students to play a game of "What's Missing?" Have one player draw a circle, think of a challenge word, and write a blank for each letter. Other players take turns guessing letters to spell the word. For every wrong guess, players have to add a part to the circle to make a face.

Grade 4/Unit 5
The Rajah's Rice

 20

Words with /əl/ and /ən/

Proofreading Activity
There are six spelling mistakes in this letter. Circle the misspelled words. Write the words correctly on the lines below.

Dear Uncel Louie,

Well, it took severel hours, but we finally arrived at the math fair. What a terribel trip! Now we're having fun, though. I saw a modle that showed the power of doubling. I used my pencal to do some simpel doubling. Well, it looked easy, but it sure wasn't! My final answer was wrong—the total was twice as great!
See you soon.

Love,
Charles

1. _____ 3. _____ 5. _____

2. _____ 4. _____ 6. _____

Writing Activity
Math is a powerful tool. You probably don't trick a Rajah out of rice with your math skills, but you do use math a lot in your everyday life. List some ways that you use math. Use four spelling words.

_____

_____

_____

_____

Words with /əl/ and /ən/

Look at the words in each set below. One word in each set is spelled correctly. Use a pencil to fill in the circle next to the correct word. Before you begin, look at the sample sets of words. Sample A has been done for you. Do Sample B by yourself. When you are sure you know what to do, you may go on with the rest of the page.

Sample A
- Ⓐ tertle
- Ⓑ tirtle
- Ⓒ turttle
- ● turtle

Sample B
- Ⓔ world
- Ⓕ wurld
- Ⓖ wirld
- Ⓗ werld

1.
- Ⓐ gentle
- Ⓑ gentil
- Ⓒ gental
- Ⓓ gentel

6.
- Ⓔ evil
- Ⓕ eval
- Ⓖ evle
- Ⓗ evle

11.
- Ⓐ womon
- Ⓑ womun
- Ⓒ women
- Ⓓ womn

16.
- Ⓔ terribel
- Ⓕ terribil
- Ⓖ terrible
- Ⓗ terribal

2.
- Ⓔ totle
- Ⓕ totel
- Ⓖ total
- Ⓗ totil

7.
- Ⓐ liston
- Ⓑ listn
- Ⓒ listen
- Ⓓ listan

12.
- Ⓔ reason
- Ⓕ reasen
- Ⓖ reasan
- Ⓗ reasin

17.
- Ⓐ several
- Ⓑ severle
- Ⓒ severel
- Ⓓ severil

3.
- Ⓐ settel
- Ⓑ settle
- Ⓒ settal
- Ⓓ settil

8.
- Ⓔ commen
- Ⓕ common
- Ⓖ comman
- Ⓗ commun

13.
- Ⓐ takon
- Ⓑ takan
- Ⓒ taken
- Ⓓ takun

18.
- Ⓔ model
- Ⓕ modle
- Ⓖ modil
- Ⓗ modle

4.
- Ⓔ medicle
- Ⓕ medicil
- Ⓖ medical
- Ⓗ medicle

9.
- Ⓐ cotten
- Ⓑ cottun
- Ⓒ cottan
- Ⓓ cotton

14.
- Ⓔ lion
- Ⓕ lyen
- Ⓖ lian
- Ⓗ liun

19.
- Ⓐ uncel
- Ⓑ uncile
- Ⓒ uncal
- Ⓓ uncle

5.
- Ⓐ leval
- Ⓑ levil
- Ⓒ level
- Ⓓ levle

10.
- Ⓔ simpel
- Ⓕ simple
- Ⓖ simpal
- Ⓗ simpil

15.
- Ⓐ pencal
- Ⓑ pencil
- Ⓒ pencle
- Ⓓ pencel

20.
- Ⓔ finel
- Ⓕ finle
- Ⓖ final
- Ⓗ finil

Contractions

Fold back the paper along the dotted line. Use the blanks to write each word as it is read aloud. When you finish the test, unfold the paper. Use the list at the right to correct any spelling mistakes. Practice the words you missed for the Posttest.

To Parents
Here are the results of your child's weekly spelling Pretest. You can help your child study for the Posttest by following these simple steps for each word on the word list:

1. Read the word to your child.

2. Have your child write the word, saying each letter as it is written.

3. Say each letter of the word as your child checks the spelling.

4. If a mistake has been made, have your child read each letter of the correctly spelled word aloud, then repeat steps 1–3.

#		#	
1.	_____	1.	that's
2.	_____	2.	he'll
3.	_____	3.	wasn't
4.	_____	4.	what's
5.	_____	5.	I'd
6.	_____	6.	there's
7.	_____	7.	couldn't
8.	_____	8.	he'd
9.	_____	9.	could've
10.	_____	10.	let's
11.	_____	11.	they'll
12.	_____	12.	weren't
13.	_____	13.	here's
14.	_____	14.	she'd
15.	_____	15.	who's
16.	_____	16.	it'll
17.	_____	17.	hadn't
18.	_____	18.	they'd
19.	_____	19.	where's
20.	_____	20.	wouldn't

Challenge Words

_____ beloved

_____ desire

_____ heaved

_____ marveled

_____ permit

Contractions

Using the Word Study Steps

1. LOOK at the word.

2. SAY the word aloud.

3. STUDY the letters in the word.

4. WRITE the word.

5. CHECK the word.

   Did you spell the word right?
   If not, go back to step 1.

Spelling Tip

When you're contracting two words, put an apostrophe in the space where the letter or letters has been lost. For example:

does + not = doesn't
it + is = it's
you + have = you've

Short Stuff

Write the spelling word contraction that is formed from the words below:

1. she would _____
2. he would _____
3. had not _____
4. here is _____
5. would not _____
6. I would _____
7. could have _____
8. let us _____
9. it will _____
10. he will _____

11. here is _____
12. where is _____
13. was not _____
14. who is _____
15. were not _____
16. that is _____
17. they would _____
18. could not _____
19. what is _____
20. they will _____

To Parents or Helpers

   Using the Word Study Steps above as your child comes across any new words will help him or her learn to spell words effectively. Review the steps as you both go over this week's spelling words.
   Go over the Spelling Tip with your child. Help your child form contractions and practice using an apostrophe to replace missing letters.
   Help your child complete the spelling activity by matching the contractions to the words they replace.

Contractions

that's	I'd	could've	here's	hadn't
he'll	there's	let's	she'd	they'd
wasn't	couldn't	they'll	who's	where's
what's	he'd	weren't	it'll	wouldn't

Patterns Plus

This week's spelling words are contractions. Write the spelling words that match these patterns:

's

1. _____
2. _____
3. _____
4. _____
5. _____
6. _____
7. _____

'll

13. _____
14. _____
15. _____

've

20. _____

n't

8. _____
9. _____
10. _____
11. _____
12. _____

'd

16. _____
17. _____
18. _____
19. _____

Contractions

that's	I'd	could've	here's	hadn't
he'll	there's	let's	she'd	they'd
wasn't	couldn't	they'll	who's	where's
what's	he'd	weren't	it'll	wouldn't

What's the Word?
Complete the paragraph by filling in each blank with a spelling word.

_____ like to play baseball, if only it _____ so muddy today. I _____ played yesterday, but I _____ find enough people to make a team. _____ play baseball anyway. _____ the ball. _____ on first base? _____ the score?

That team is so good, _____ win for sure. Jimmy is up to bat; I know that _____ hit a home run. _____ the pitch. I knew _____ swing! _____ a hit! _____ be a home run. I _____ miss this exciting game for anything!

And Then . . .
What happened to Yeh-Shen ten years after the story ended? Write a paragraph telling what her life is like. Use the spelling words *hadn't*, *weren't*, *they'd*, *where's*, and *she'd* as you describe her life.

_____

_____

_____

_____

150

Challenge Extension: Have students write fill-in sentences for each challenge word. Then have each student exchange papers with a partner and see how many sentences the other student can correctly fill in.

Grade 4/Unit 5
Yeh-Shen | 20 |

Contractions

Proofreading Activity

There are six spelling mistakes in this book review. Circle the misspelled words.
Write the words correctly on the lines below.

Id like to recommend the story "Yeh-Shen" because it is very interesting. You
would'nt believe what happens! Ther'es a beautiful girl named Yeh-Shen who
was'nt treated fairly by her stepmother. Sh'ed have to do all the chores and
could'nt have any fun. It'll keep you reading to the very end!

1. _____ 3. _____ 5. _____

2. _____ 4. _____ 6. _____

Writing Activity

Write your own fairy tale about wonderful events and fascinating characters.
Make sure the evil people are punished and the good people are rewarded. Use
four spelling words.

_____

_____

_____

_____

Contractions

Look at the words in each set below. One word in each set is spelled correctly. Use a pencil to fill in the circle next to the correct word. Before you begin, look at the sample sets of words. Sample A has been done for you. Do Sample B by yourself. When you are sure you know what to do, you may go on with the rest of the page.

Sample A
- Ⓐ haveen't
- Ⓑ have'nt
- Ⓒ haven't
- Ⓓ havent

Sample B
- Ⓔ she'll
- Ⓕ she'ill
- Ⓖ shel'l
- Ⓗ shee'll

1.
- Ⓐ itll
- Ⓑ it'll
- Ⓒ itl'l
- Ⓓ i'tll

2.
- Ⓔ she'd
- Ⓕ shee'd
- Ⓖ sh'ed
- Ⓗ she'dd

3.
- Ⓐ whos
- Ⓑ wh'os
- Ⓒ who's
- Ⓓ who'se

4.
- Ⓔ hadnt
- Ⓕ had'nt
- Ⓖ hadd'nt
- Ⓗ hadn't

5.
- Ⓐ theyd
- Ⓑ they'd
- Ⓒ the'yd
- Ⓓ the'dy

6.
- Ⓔ wheres
- Ⓕ whe'res
- Ⓖ where's
- Ⓗ wher'es

7.
- Ⓐ wouldn't
- Ⓑ wouldnt
- Ⓒ would'nt
- Ⓓ woul'dnt

8.
- Ⓔ Id
- Ⓕ Id'
- Ⓖ I'de
- Ⓗ I'd

9.
- Ⓐ theres
- Ⓑ the'res
- Ⓒ there's
- Ⓓ ther'es

10.
- Ⓔ couldnt
- Ⓕ couldn't
- Ⓖ could'nt
- Ⓗ coul'dnt

11.
- Ⓐ he'd
- Ⓑ hed
- Ⓒ he'ed
- Ⓓ he'ad

12.
- Ⓔ werent
- Ⓕ weren't
- Ⓖ wer'ent
- Ⓗ were'nt

13.
- Ⓐ heres
- Ⓑ her'es
- Ⓒ here's
- Ⓓ he'res

14.
- Ⓔ couldve
- Ⓕ coul'dve
- Ⓖ couldv'e
- Ⓗ could've

15.
- Ⓐ lets
- Ⓑ le'ts
- Ⓒ let's
- Ⓓ let'us

16.
- Ⓔ theyll
- Ⓕ theyl'l
- Ⓖ they'll
- Ⓗ the'yll

17.
- Ⓐ whats
- Ⓑ what'is
- Ⓒ what's
- Ⓓ wh'ats

18.
- Ⓔ wasn't
- Ⓕ wasnt
- Ⓖ was'nt
- Ⓗ was'snt

19.
- Ⓐ hel'l
- Ⓑ he'll
- Ⓒ he'ill
- Ⓓ he'will

20.
- Ⓔ thats
- Ⓕ tha'ts
- Ⓖ thats'
- Ⓗ that's

Words from Science

Fold back the paper along the dotted line. Use the blanks to write each word as it is read aloud. When you finish the test, unfold the paper. Use the list at the right to correct any spelling mistakes. Practice the words you missed for the Posttest.

To Parents

Here are the results of your child's weekly spelling Pretest. You can help your child study for the Posttest by following these simple steps for each word on the word list:

1. Read the word to your child.

2. Have your child write the word, saying each letter as it is written.

3. Say each letter of the word as your child checks the spelling.

4. If a mistake has been made, have your child read each letter of the correctly spelled word aloud, then repeat steps 1–3.

1. _____
2. _____
3. _____
4. _____
5. _____
6. _____
7. _____
8. _____
9. _____
10. _____
11. _____
12. _____
13. _____
14. _____
15. _____
16. _____
17. _____
18. _____
19. _____
20. _____

1. rescue
2. survive
3. channel
4. vessel
5. expose
6. dying
7. shelter
8. extreme
9. danger
10. protect
11. seaweed
12. creatures
13. dissolve
14. motion
15. feature
16. adapt
17. locate
18. assist
19. future
20. divers

Challenge Words

_____
_____
_____
_____
_____

coral

damage

loosened

percent

reefs

Words from Science

Using the Word Study Steps

1. LOOK at the word.

2. SAY the word aloud.

3. STUDY the letters in the word.

4. WRITE the word.

5. CHECK the word.

    Did you spell the word right?
    If not, go back to step 1.

Spelling Tip

Accented syllables are spoken with more force than unaccented ones.

Pronouncing a word correctly can help you spell it correctly.

Unscramble each set of letters to make a spelling word.

1. rueesc _____

2. vivesur _____

3. nnelach _____

4. slesve _____

5. eosexp _____

6. ingdy _____

7. reeltsh _____

8. meeextr _____

9. gerand _____

10. tepctro _____

11. wdeease _____

12. eesuratcr _____

13. edolviss _____

14. itonmo _____

15. taureef _____

16. tapad _____

17. ceatlo _____

18. sistas _____

19. treufu _____

20. servdi _____

To Parents or Helpers

   Using the Word Study Steps above as your child comes across any new words will help him or her learn to spell words effectively. Review the steps as you both go over this week's spelling words.

   Go over the Spelling Tip with your child. Help your child look up the spelling words in a dictionary to find the accented syllables.

   Help your child complete the spelling activity by unscrambling each spelling word.

Words from Science

rescue	expose	danger	dissolve	locate
survive	dying	protect	motion	assist
channel	shelter	seaweed	feature	future
vessel	extreme	creatures	adapt	divers

Accent on the Syllable

Use a dictionary to help you sort the spelling words according to the placement of the accent.

Accented First Syllable

1. _____   8. _____

2. _____   9. _____

3. _____   10. _____

4. _____   11. _____

5. _____   12. _____

6. _____   13. _____

7. _____

Accented Second Syllable

14. _____   18. _____

15. _____   19. _____

16. _____   20. _____

17. _____

Words from Science

rescue	expose	danger	dissolve	locate
survive	dying	protect	motion	assist
channel	shelter	seaweed	feature	future
vessel	extreme	creatures	adapt	divers

Meaning Match

Write the spelling word that matches each clue below.

1. coming _____

2. reveal _____

3. animals _____

4. hazard _____

5. severe _____

6. help _____

7. find _____

8. keep from harm _____

9. adjust _____

10. ship _____

11. place of safety _____

12. exist _____

13. movement _____

14. kelp _____

15. save _____

Sentence Derby

Use each word in a sentence.

16. channel _____

17. dying _____

18. dissolve _____

19. feature _____

20. divers _____

Challenge Extension: Students can draw pictures of
things they could find on a reef and caption each picture
with sentences that use one or more Challenge Words.

Words from Science

Proofreading Activity

There are six spelling mistakes in this script for a speech. Circle the misspelled words. Write the words correctly on the lines below.

Ladies and Gentlemen:

The reefs are in extreame danger of dyinng! We must protect the seawead and other creetures on the reef. We must work together to resceu the reefs or they will not surrvive! Please assist me, so the reefs will be a part of our future.

1. _____ 3. _____ 5. _____

2. _____ 4. _____ 6. _____

Writing Activity

What did you learn about the reefs? Write four more facts to add to the "Reef Facts" at the end of the selection. Use four spelling words.

_____

_____

_____

_____

Words from Science

Look at the words in each set below. One word in each set is spelled correctly. Use a pencil to fill in the circle next to the correct word. Before you begin, look at the sample sets of words. Sample A has been done for you. Do Sample B by yourself. When you are sure you know what to do, you may go on with the rest of the page.

Sample A
- Ⓐ science ●
- Ⓑ sience
- Ⓒ sciense
- Ⓓ siense

Sample B
- Ⓔ natuve
- Ⓕ native
- Ⓖ nativ
- Ⓗ nattive

1.
- Ⓐ divars
- Ⓑ divers
- Ⓒ diverrs
- Ⓓ divurs

6.
- Ⓔ feture
- Ⓕ fature
- Ⓖ feature
- Ⓗ featere

11.
- Ⓐ moton
- Ⓑ motion
- Ⓒ motoin
- Ⓓ mottion

16.
- Ⓔ chanel
- Ⓕ channel
- Ⓖ channal
- Ⓗ chanal

2.
- Ⓔ futture
- Ⓕ futere
- Ⓖ future
- Ⓗ futare

7.
- Ⓐ loccate
- Ⓑ locatte
- Ⓒ locate
- Ⓓ lacate

12.
- Ⓔ expose
- Ⓕ exppose
- Ⓖ exposse
- Ⓗ expuse

17.
- Ⓐ extreme
- Ⓑ extereme
- Ⓒ extrame
- Ⓓ exterame

3.
- Ⓐ assist
- Ⓑ asist
- Ⓒ assisst
- Ⓓ assast

8.
- Ⓔ protect
- Ⓕ prottect
- Ⓖ protact
- Ⓗ protecct

13.
- Ⓐ dyng
- Ⓑ dying
- Ⓒ dyinng
- Ⓓ dyiing

18.
- Ⓔ surrvive
- Ⓕ survvive
- Ⓖ survive
- Ⓗ survave

4.
- Ⓔ sheter
- Ⓕ sheler
- Ⓖ shellter
- Ⓗ shelter

9.
- Ⓐ disolve
- Ⓑ dissollve
- Ⓒ dissalve
- Ⓓ dissolve

14.
- Ⓔ seeweed
- Ⓕ seawed
- Ⓖ seaweed
- Ⓗ seawweed

19.
- Ⓐ vesel
- Ⓑ vessal
- Ⓒ vessel
- Ⓓ vessell

5.
- Ⓐ adupt
- Ⓑ addapt
- Ⓒ adappt
- Ⓓ adapt

10.
- Ⓔ creatares
- Ⓕ creatures
- Ⓖ creattures
- Ⓗ cretures

15.
- Ⓐ dangur
- Ⓑ dangar
- Ⓒ dangger
- Ⓓ danger

20.
- Ⓔ rescu
- Ⓕ resscue
- Ⓖ recue
- Ⓗ rescue

Name_____ Date_____

Grade 4/Unit 5 Review Test

Read each sentence. If an underlined word is spelled wrong, fill in the circle that goes with that word. If no word is spelled wrong, fill in the circle below NONE. Read Sample A, and do Sample B.

A. I will <u>trade</u> my <u>bat</u> for a <u>bike</u>.
       A   B   C

NONE
A. Ⓐ Ⓑ Ⓒ ●

B. My <u>sister</u> carries her <u>books</u> to <u>skool</u>.
      E   F   G

NONE
B. Ⓔ Ⓕ Ⓖ Ⓗ

1. The <u>women</u> heard the <u>gentel</u> <u>laughter</u>.
       A   B   C

NONE
1. Ⓐ Ⓑ Ⓒ Ⓓ

2. <u>Soler</u> power <u>could've</u> been an <u>enormous</u> aid.
    E   F   G

NONE
2. Ⓔ Ⓕ Ⓖ Ⓗ

3. A <u>citizen</u> helps <u>natur</u> by using <u>solar</u> heating.
      A   B   C

NONE
3. Ⓐ Ⓑ Ⓒ Ⓓ

4. <u>He'll</u> need <u>advice</u> to <u>triump</u> in war.
    E   F   G

NONE
4. Ⓔ Ⓕ Ⓖ Ⓗ

5. The <u>women</u> like <u>either</u> <u>cotton</u> or wool coats.
      A   B   C

NONE
5. Ⓐ Ⓑ Ⓒ Ⓓ

6. I see <u>several</u> <u>tendur</u> shoots from <u>cotton</u> plants.
        E   F   G

NONE
6. Ⓔ Ⓕ Ⓖ Ⓗ

7. <u>The'yd</u> dropped the <u>anchor</u> to <u>protect</u> the ship.
    A   B   C

NONE
7. Ⓐ Ⓑ Ⓒ Ⓓ

8. Use <u>ether</u> a blue or green <u>pencil</u> to draw <u>seaweed</u>.
      E   F   G

NONE
8. Ⓔ Ⓕ Ⓖ Ⓗ

9. <u>Who's</u> going to <u>assist</u> the old <u>women</u>?
    A   B   C

NONE
9. Ⓐ Ⓑ Ⓒ Ⓓ

10. <u>Hadn't</u> we best <u>protect</u> our <u>dyeing</u> rain forests?
     E   F   G

NONE
10. Ⓔ Ⓕ Ⓖ Ⓗ

11. Helping a whale to <u>survive</u> is an <u>enormus</u> <u>triumph</u>.
                A   B   C

NONE
11. Ⓐ Ⓑ Ⓒ Ⓓ

Grade 4 Unit 5 Review Test

12. He'll join several others by becoming a sitizen.
     E   F   G

NONE
12. Ⓔ   Ⓕ   Ⓖ   Ⓗ

13. The laughter is dying down. Now h'ell speak.
              A   B   C

NONE
13. Ⓐ   Ⓑ   Ⓒ   Ⓓ

14. The gentle rain could've covered the anchor.
              E   F   G

NONE
14. Ⓔ   Ⓕ   Ⓖ   Ⓗ

15. Please asist nature to help plants survive.
                  A   B   C

NONE
15. Ⓐ   Ⓑ   Ⓒ   Ⓓ

16. They'd tried to proteck the dying bird.
        E   F   G

NONE
16. Ⓔ   Ⓕ   Ⓖ   Ⓗ

17. A citizen writes with either a pencil or a pen.
            A   B   C

NONE
17. Ⓐ   Ⓑ   Ⓒ   Ⓓ

18. Boil seaweed several minutes to make it tendur.
              E   F   G

NONE
18. Ⓔ   Ⓕ   Ⓖ   Ⓗ

19. Wh'os going to assist him by giving advice?
        A   B   C

NONE
19. Ⓐ   Ⓑ   Ⓒ   Ⓓ

20. They'd rather you hadin't given them advice.
        E   F   G

NONE
20. Ⓔ   Ⓕ   Ⓖ   Ⓗ

21. Who's going to use that enormous pensil?
        A   B   C

NONE
21. Ⓐ   Ⓑ   Ⓒ   Ⓓ

22. Can seaweed survive under that ancor?
              E   F   G

NONE
22. Ⓔ   Ⓕ   Ⓖ   Ⓗ

23. Solar energy will help nature triumph.
        A   B   C

NONE
23. Ⓐ   Ⓑ   Ⓒ   Ⓓ

24. I hadn't yet heard the babies' tender laffter.
          E   F   G

NONE
24. Ⓔ   Ⓕ   Ⓖ   Ⓗ

25. I could've worn my soft, gentle, cotten scarf.
            A   B   C

NONE
25. Ⓐ   Ⓑ   Ⓒ   Ⓓ

Words with Silent Letters

Pretest Directions
Fold back the paper along the dotted line. Use the blanks to write each word as it is read aloud. When you finish the test, unfold the paper. Use the list at the right to correct any spelling mistakes. Practice the words you missed for the Posttest.

To Parents
Here are the results of your child's weekly spelling Pretest. You can help your child study for the Posttest by following these simple steps for each word on the word list:

1. Read the word to your child.

2. Have your child write the word, saying each letter as it is written.

3. Say each letter of the word as your child checks the spelling.

4. If a mistake has been made, have your child read each letter of the correctly spelled word aloud, and then repeat steps 1–3.

1. _____ 1. knew
2. _____ 2. climb
3. _____ 3. calm
4. _____ 4. although
5. _____ 5. knight
6. _____ 6. writer
7. _____ 7. knob
8. _____ 8. numb
9. _____ 9. delight
10. _____ 10. wren
11. _____ 11. knead
12. _____ 12. plumber
13. _____ 13. chalk
14. _____ 14. midnight
15. _____ 15. wreck
16. _____ 16. stalk
17. _____ 17. kneel
18. _____ 18. sought
19. _____ 19 thorough
20. _____ 20. wrestle

Challenge Words

_____ circulated
_____ extraordinary
_____ launched
_____ opponents
_____ organizations

Name_____ Date_____

Words with Silent Letters

Using the Word Study Steps

1. LOOK at the word.

2. SAY the word aloud.

3. STUDY the letters in the word.

4. WRITE the word.

5. CHECK the word.

Did you spell the word right?
If not, go back to step 1.

Spelling Tips

Silent letters may come at the beginning, in the middle, or at the end of a word. For example:
beginning: <u>k</u>nob
middle: deli<u>gh</u>t
end: num<u>b</u>

Find Rhyming Words

Rhyming words have the same last sound. Circle the word in each row that has the same last sound as the spelling word on the left.

1.	knew	kneel	few	11.	chalk	chart	walk
2.	climb	rhyme	limb	12.	wreck	deck	wrench
3.	although	grow	enough	13.	kneel	knot	wheel
4.	knight	bright	knit	14.	sought	bought	laughed
5.	writer	written	brighter	15.	thorough	sorrow	tough
6.	knob	knee	job	16.	calm	calf	palm
7.	numb	plum	number	17.	plumber	summer	plus
8.	delight	write	delay	18.	midnight	white	middle
9.	wren	wrote	when	19.	stalk	step	hawk
10.	knead	seed	nod	20.	wrestle	wring	nestle

To Parents or Helpers

Using the Word Study Steps above as your child comes across any new words will help him or her learn to spell words effectively. Review the steps as you both go over this week's spelling words.

Go over the Spelling Tip with your child. Help him or her find the silent letters in each of this week's spelling words.

Help your child complete the spelling activity.

Words with Silent Letters

knew	knight	delight	chalk	kneel
climb	writer	wren	midnight	sought
calm	knob	knead	wreck	thorough
although	numb	plumber	stalk	wrestle

Pattern Power!

Write the spelling words with these spelling patterns.

words with silent *k*

1. _____
2. _____
3. _____
4. _____
5. _____

words with silent *b*

6. _____
7. _____
8. _____

words with silent *l*

9. _____
10. _____
11. _____

words with silent *gh*

12. _____
13. _____
14. _____
15. _____
16. _____

words with silent *w*

17. _____
18. _____
19. _____
20. _____

Words with Silent Letters

knew	knight	delight	chalk	kneel
climb	writer	wren	midnight	sought
calm	knob	knead	wreck	thorough
although	numb	plumber	stalk	wrestle

What's the Word?
Complete each sentence with a word from the spelling list.

1. This book was written by my favorite _____.

2. His hiking boots helped him _____ the steep hill.

3. The jacket still fits, _____ I've grown a bit.

4. She turned the _____ of the door.

5. My fingers became so cold, they felt _____.

6. A tiny _____ built a nest in the bird house.

7. We had to call a _____ to come and fix the leak.

8. A cat will first _____ a mouse before catching one.

9. Tom is learning to _____ in the gym after school.

10. They _____ an answer to the problem.

11. The _____ broke when he used it on the chalkboard.

12. When I heard the phone ring, I _____ it was you.

Opposites
Write the spelling word that is opposite in meaning to the words below.

13. nervous _____   16. build _____

14. sadness _____   17. stand _____

15. noon _____   18. incomplete _____

Challenge Extension: Write a fill-in sentence for each Challenge Word. Exchange papers with a partner and complete each other's fill-in sentences.

Grade 4/Unit 6
Teammates 18

Words with Silent Letters

Proofreading

There are six spelling mistakes in the paragraph below. Circle the misspelled words. Write the words correctly on the lines below.

"Oh, no!" Coach said, as he twisted the nob to turn off the water. "The sink in the team bathroom is leaking again." My Aunt Mary is a plummer, so we asked her to fix the sink. It was hard to find the leak. Aunt Mary had to neal on the hard tile floor until her knees were nubm. After finding the leak, she went to the store to buy a new pipe. Aunt Mary had to restle with the new pipe to get it in place. "There!" Aunt Mary said, smiling with delite. "The sink is fixed."

1. _____ 3. _____ 5. _____

2. _____ 4. _____ 6. _____

Writing Activity

What team sport do you like to play or to watch? Write a few sentences about your favorite sport. Use four spelling words in your writing.

_____

_____

_____

_____

Words with Silent Letters

Look at the words in each set below. One word in each set is spelled correctly. Use a pencil to fill in the circle next to the correct word. Before you begin, look at the sample sets of words. Sample A has been done for you. Do Sample B by yourself. When you are sure you know what to do, you may go on with the rest of the page.

Sample A
- Ⓐ crum
- 🄱 crumb
- Ⓒ crubm
- Ⓓ crume

Sample B
- Ⓔ known
- Ⓕ nowne
- Ⓖ knon
- Ⓗ nown

1.
- Ⓐ kned
- Ⓑ knead
- Ⓒ nead
- Ⓓ knede

2.
- Ⓔ numb
- Ⓕ num
- Ⓖ numm
- Ⓗ nubm

3.
- Ⓐ midnite
- Ⓑ midnigt
- Ⓒ midnight
- Ⓓ midnighte

4.
- Ⓔ restle
- Ⓕ wresle
- Ⓖ wrastle
- Ⓗ wrestle

5.
- Ⓐ calm
- Ⓑ caml
- Ⓒ camm
- Ⓓ colm

6.
- Ⓔ plumer
- Ⓕ plummer
- Ⓖ plumber
- Ⓗ plummber

7.
- Ⓐ neel
- Ⓑ kneel
- Ⓒ kneal
- Ⓓ neal

8.
- Ⓔ knite
- Ⓕ knight
- Ⓖ knigt
- Ⓗ nite

9.
- Ⓐ althogh
- Ⓑ althouh
- Ⓒ although
- Ⓓ althoe

10.
- Ⓔ delight
- Ⓕ delite
- Ⓖ deliht
- Ⓗ deelight

11.
- Ⓐ reck
- Ⓑ wrek
- Ⓒ wreck
- Ⓓ wrecke

12.
- Ⓔ souhgt
- Ⓕ suoght
- Ⓖ saught
- Ⓗ sought

13.
- Ⓐ knew
- Ⓑ kneu
- Ⓒ nkew
- Ⓓ newe

14.
- Ⓔ thorogh
- Ⓕ thorough
- Ⓖ throgh
- Ⓗ thorow

15.
- Ⓐ chak
- Ⓑ chalk
- Ⓒ chaulk
- Ⓓ chawk

16.
- Ⓔ nahb
- Ⓕ nkob
- Ⓖ knab
- Ⓗ knob

17.
- Ⓐ cliem
- Ⓑ climb
- Ⓒ clim
- Ⓓ clyme

18.
- Ⓔ staulk
- Ⓕ stauk
- Ⓖ stalk
- Ⓗ stawk

19.
- Ⓐ writer
- Ⓑ writter
- Ⓒ riter
- Ⓓ wrighter

20.
- Ⓔ renn
- Ⓕ wren
- Ⓖ wern
- Ⓗ wrene

Homophones and Homographs

Pretest Directions

Fold back the paper along the dotted line. Use the blanks to write each word as it is said aloud. When you finish the test, unfold the paper. Use the list at the right to correct any spelling mistakes. Practice the words that you missed for the Posttest.

To Parents

Here are the results of your child's weekly spelling Pretest. You can help your child study for the Posttest by following these simple steps for each word on the word list:

1. Read the word to your child.

2. Have your child write the word, saying each letter as it is written.

3. Say each letter of the word as your child checks the spelling.

4. If a mistake has been made, have your child read each letter of the correctly spelled word aloud and then repeat steps 1–3.

#		Word
1.	_____	1. seen
2.	_____	2. great
3.	_____	3. light
4.	_____	4. beat
5.	_____	5. lean
6.	_____	6. scene
7.	_____	7. beet
8.	_____	8. bowl
9.	_____	9. grate
10.	_____	10. fan
11.	_____	11. peak
12.	_____	12. post
13.	_____	13. pail
14.	_____	14. bury
15.	_____	15. punch
16.	_____	16. pale
17.	_____	17. grave
18.	_____	18. berry
19.	_____	19 peek
20.	_____	20. dates

Challenge Words

_____ feeble

_____ fragrance

_____ mingled

_____ resembled

_____ scampered

Homophones and Homographs

Using the Word Study Steps

1. LOOK at the word.

2. SAY the word aloud.

3. STUDY the letters in the word.

4. WRITE the word.

5. CHECK the word.

   Did you spell the word right?
   If not, go back to step 1.

Spelling Tips

Homophones are English words that sound alike but are spelled differently.

For example: Jill looked <u>pale</u> as she tumbled after Jack while holding her <u>pail</u>.

Homographs are English words that are spelled the same but mean different things.

For example: This lamp is <u>light</u> to carry and can <u>light</u> up the room.

Find and Circle

Circle the 20 spelling words. Be careful! Some of the spelling words run up and down or diagonally.

l	g	r	a	t	e	r	m	g	l	p	o	s	t	b
a	r	b	e	r	r	y	e	r	p	a	i	l	o	r
d	a	t	e	s	c	e	n	e	p	l	i	g	h	t
l	v	p	s	a	e	r	w	a	f	e	m	o	s	b
p	e	e	f	t	t	e	r	t	u	b	e	e	t	u
j	i	a	a	l	p	u	n	c	h	o	c	k	a	r
a	z	k	n	e	r	l	i	e	b	o	w	l	m	y

To Parents or Helpers

Using the Word Study Steps above as your child comes across any new words will help him or her spell well. Review the steps as you both go over this week's spelling words.

Go over the Spelling Tip with your child. Help him or her think of sentences using each of this week's spelling words.

Help your child complete the spelling activity.

Homophones and Homographs

seen	lean	grate	pail	grave
great	scene	fan	bury	berry
light	beet	peak	punch	peek
beat	bowl	post	pale	dates

There are six pairs of spelling words that are homophones. They sound the same but are spelled differently. Sort the homophones into pairs. Write each pair on the lines below.

1. _____ _____   4. _____ _____

2. _____ _____   5. _____ _____

3. _____ _____   6. _____ _____

Eight spelling words are homographs. Homographs are words that are spelled the same, but that have different meanings. Using a dictionary, write two different meanings for each spelling word below.

1. light

   meaning 1._____

   meaning 2._____

2. lean

   meaning 1._____

   meaning 2._____

3. bowl

   meaning 1._____

   meaning 2._____

4. fan

   meaning 1._____

   meaning 2._____

5. post

   meaning 1._____

   meaning 2._____

6. punch

   meaning 1._____

   meaning 2._____

7. grave

   meaning 1._____

   meaning 2._____

8. dates

   meaning 1._____

   meaning 2._____

Homophones and Homographs

seen	lean	grate	pail	grave
great	scene	fan	bury	berry
light	beet	peak	punch	peek
beat	bowl	post	pale	dates

Complete each sentence below with a spelling word.

1. Close your eyes and don't _____.

2. Have you _____ the movie that just opened?

3. Please _____ the carrots for the salad.

4. I say three lines in _____ one of the play.

5. She likes to eat dried, sweet _____ for dessert.

6. That carton is _____ enough for me to carry myself.

7. They climbed to the _____ of the mountain.

8. I use suntan lotion because I have _____ skin.

9. Let's _____ the treasure in the backyard.

10. Mix the batter in a large mixing _____.

11. He carried the water in a large _____.

12. I am a big _____ of the Dallas Cowboys football team.

Word Meaning: Analogies

Write the spelling word that fits the analogy.

1. _____ is to *terrific* as *bad* is to *awful*.

2. *Vegetable* is to _____ as *meat* is to *steak*.

3. _____ is to *serious* as *happy* is to *glad*.

4. *Tall* is to *short* as *fat* is to _____.

Challenge Extension: Write a fill-in sentence for each Challenge
Word. Exchange papers with a partner and complete the sentences.

170

Grade 4/Unit 6
The Malachite Palace 16

Homophones and Homographs

Proofreading Activity

There are six spelling mistakes in the paragraph below. Circle the misspelled words. Write the words correctly on the lines below.

Though Jason was a prince, he had never scene the top of a mountain before. This day, he decided to climb a mountain. He stood on the peek and saw the whole country. The lite of the sun shone on the valleys below. It was very beautiful. After a while, Jason became hungry. He munched on some delicious dats and drank some sweet punche. When the sun began to set, Jason started down the mountain toward home. That night, in bed, Jason thought about the grate time he'd had that day. He promised himself that he would climb the mountain again soon.

1. _____   3. _____   5. _____

2. _____   4. _____   6. _____

Writing Activity

Think of a place you would like to see. Write a few sentences about what you would see or do there. Use four spelling words in your writing.

_____

_____

_____

_____

Homophones and Homographs

Posttest Directions

Look at the words in each set below. One word in each set is spelled correctly. Use a pencil to fill in the circle next to the correct word. Before you begin, look at the sample sets of words. Sample A has been done for you. Do Sample B by yourself. When you are sure you know what to do, you may go on with the rest of the page.

Sample A
- Ⓐ stear
- Ⓑ starr
- ⬤ stare
- Ⓓ starre

Sample B
- Ⓔ ritte
- Ⓕ rite
- Ⓖ righte
- Ⓗ right

1.
- Ⓐ seen
- Ⓑ sene
- Ⓒ sein
- Ⓓ seene

2.
- Ⓔ bete
- Ⓕ beate
- Ⓖ beete
- Ⓗ beat

3.
- Ⓐ peke
- Ⓑ peek
- Ⓒ peake
- Ⓓ peeke

4.
- Ⓔ peale
- Ⓕ pael
- Ⓖ pail
- Ⓗ paile

5.
- Ⓐ bury
- Ⓑ burry
- Ⓒ bure
- Ⓓ burie

6.
- Ⓔ leit
- Ⓕ lighte
- Ⓖ light
- Ⓗ litte

7.
- Ⓐ leen
- Ⓑ lean
- Ⓒ leane
- Ⓓ leene

8.
- Ⓔ bowl
- Ⓕ boal
- Ⓖ boall
- Ⓗ boul

9.
- Ⓐ fane
- Ⓑ fan
- Ⓒ fann
- Ⓓ fain

10.
- Ⓔ post
- Ⓕ poste
- Ⓖ potse
- Ⓗ poost

11.
- Ⓐ pnuch
- Ⓑ punch
- Ⓒ puntch
- Ⓓ panch

12.
- Ⓔ greave
- Ⓕ graive
- Ⓖ grayv
- Ⓗ grave

13.
- Ⓐ daets
- Ⓑ deates
- Ⓒ dates
- Ⓓ daits

14.
- Ⓔ great
- Ⓕ graet
- Ⓖ grayt
- Ⓗ grait

15.
- Ⓐ scean
- Ⓑ scene
- Ⓒ seene
- Ⓓ seine

16.
- Ⓔ beete
- Ⓕ beate
- Ⓖ beit
- Ⓗ beet

17.
- Ⓐ grate
- Ⓑ greate
- Ⓒ graet
- Ⓓ grayte

18.
- Ⓔ peake
- Ⓕ peak
- Ⓖ peeke
- Ⓗ paik

19.
- Ⓐ paile
- Ⓑ pael
- Ⓒ pale
- Ⓓ plael

20.
- Ⓔ berri
- Ⓕ berry
- Ⓖ bery
- Ⓗ berrye

Words with Suffixes

Pretest Directions

Fold back the paper along the dotted line. Use the blanks to write each word as it is read aloud. When you finish the test, unfold the paper. Use the list at the right to correct any spelling mistakes. Practice the words that you missed for the Posttest.

To Parents

Here are the results of your child's weekly spelling Pretest. You can help your child study for the Posttest by following these simple steps for each word on the word list:

1. Read the word to your child.

2. Have your child write the word, saying each letter as it is written.

3. Say each letter of the word as your child checks the spelling.

4. If a mistake has been made, have your child read each letter of the correctly spelled word aloud, and then repeat steps 1–3.

1. _____	1. useless
2. _____	2. entertainment
3. _____	3. construction
4. _____	4. adjustable
5. _____	5. darkness
6. _____	6. motionless
7. _____	7. description
8. _____	8. measurement
9. _____	9. adorable
10. _____	10. breathless
11. _____	11. fairness
12. _____	12. government
13. _____	13. protection
14. _____	14. dependable
15. _____	15. sickness
16. _____	16. hopeless
17. _____	17. production
18. _____	18. enjoyable
19. _____	19. greatness
20. _____	20. encouragement

Challenge Words

_____ brilliant

_____ commercials

_____ expensive

_____ ingredient

_____ successful

Words with Suffixes

Using the Word Study Steps

1. LOOK at the word.

2. SAY the word aloud.

3. STUDY the letters in the word.

4. WRITE the word.

5. CHECK the word.

   Did you spell the word right?
   If not, go back to step 1.

Spelling Tip

Learn how to spell suffixes you use often in writing.

-tion -ment -less

Word Scramble

Unscramble each set of letters to make a spelling word.

1. slussee _____

2. treamnentietn _____

3. stronctioucn _____

4. jablaudste _____

5. knesards _____

6. slimontose _____

7. prescinitod _____

8. mensurteame _____

9. bladoare _____

10. thasbleres _____

11. asfrnies _____

12. merntevong _____

13. oprictnote _____

14. plabdedeen _____

15. sniksecs _____

16. shlopese _____

17. upictonrod _____

18. jabloyeen _____

19. sesterang _____

20. cenroumagneet _____

To Parents or Helpers

   Using the Word Study Steps above as your child comes across any new words will help him or her learn to spell words effectively. Review the steps as you both go over this week's spelling words.

   Go over the Spelling Tip with your child. Ask your child if he or she can spell some other suffixes.

   Help your child complete the spelling activity.

Explore the Pattern

useless	darkness	adorable	protection	production
entertainment	motionless	breathless	dependable	enjoyable
construction	description	fairness	sickness	greatness
adjustable	measurement	government	hopeless	encouragement

Pattern Power

Sort each spelling word by writing it under the correct suffix.

-less

1. _____
2. _____
3. _____
4. _____

-ness

5. _____
6. _____
7. _____
8. _____

-ment

9. _____
10. _____
11. _____
12. _____

-tion

13. _____
14. _____
15. _____
16. _____

-able

17. _____
18. _____
19. _____
20. _____

Words with Suffixes

useless	darkness	adorable	protection	production
entertainment	motionless	breathless	dependable	enjoyable
construction	description	fairness	sickness	greatness
adjustable	measurement	government	hopeless	encouragement

Word Meaning: Suffixes

A suffix is added to the end of a word to give the word a different meaning. Different suffixes have different meanings. (examples: "happiness" means "the state of being happy"; "readable" means "able to be read")

-less	=	without
-ment	=	the act of
-able	=	able to be
-ness	=	the state of being
-tion	=	the act of

Write the spelling word that fits each meaning below.

1. without use _____

2. the act of constructing _____

3. able to be adjusted _____

4. the state of being dark _____

5. without breath _____

6. the act of describing _____

7. the act of measuring _____

8. without motion _____

9. able to be adored _____

10. the state of being fair _____

Challenge Extension: Have you ever seen an ad on TV? Think of an ad that you like and write about it using the Challenge Words.

Grade 4/Unit 6
The Toothpaste Millionaire
10

Words with Suffixes

Proofreading

There are six spelling mistakes in the paragraph below. Circle the misspelled words. Write the words correctly on the lines below.

I set to work to invent a time machine. Everyone said it was hopless. But I did it! I designed the machine myself. Then I got the materials I needed and began on the machine's construktion. Time travel is not like "real" travel. You and the machine are absolutely moshunless. When the machine stops and you get out, what you see is beyond diskription. Just yesterday, I visited some adorible dinosaurs. Tomorrow, I think I'd like to go to the future. Do you think the govinment would be interested in buying one of my machines?

1. _____   3. _____   5. _____

2. _____   4. _____   6. _____

Writing Activity

What would you like to invent or produce? Write a few sentences about what your invention would be like. Use four spelling words in your writing.

_____

_____

_____

_____

Words with Suffixes

Look at the words in each set. One word in each set is spelled correctly. Use a pencil to color in the circle next to the correct word. Before you begin, look at the sample sets of words. Sample A has been done for you. Do Sample B by yourself. When you are sure you know what to do, you may go on with the rest of the page.

Sample A
- Ⓐ developmint
- Ⓑ devellopmunt
- Ⓒ development
- Ⓓ divelopmunt

Sample B
- Ⓔ clooliss
- Ⓕ clueless
- Ⓖ clooless
- Ⓗ cluliss

1.
- Ⓐ adjustible
- Ⓑ adjustable
- Ⓒ adjustble
- Ⓓ ajustable

6.
- Ⓔ useless
- Ⓕ usless
- Ⓖ useles
- Ⓗ ussless

11.
- Ⓐ dependible
- Ⓑ dependble
- Ⓒ dependable
- Ⓓ dipendable

16.
- Ⓔ protection
- Ⓕ protectin
- Ⓖ protetion
- Ⓗ prutection

2.
- Ⓔ constructon
- Ⓕ constructin
- Ⓖ construction
- Ⓗ construkton

7.
- Ⓐ measurment
- Ⓑ measurement
- Ⓒ measuremint
- Ⓓ mesurement

12.
- Ⓔ discription
- Ⓕ description
- Ⓖ descriptoun
- Ⓗ deskription

17.
- Ⓐ adorble
- Ⓑ adorable
- Ⓒ adorabel
- Ⓓ adorible

3.
- Ⓐ fairness
- Ⓑ fairnes
- Ⓒ fairnese
- Ⓓ fareness

8.
- Ⓔ enjoiable
- Ⓕ enjoyble
- Ⓖ enjoyible
- Ⓗ enjoyable

13.
- Ⓐ motionless
- Ⓑ motonless
- Ⓒ motionles
- Ⓓ motunless

18.
- Ⓔ hopless
- Ⓕ hopeliss
- Ⓖ hopeless
- Ⓗ hopeles

4.
- Ⓔ breathles
- Ⓕ breatheless
- Ⓖ breathless
- Ⓗ brethliss

9.
- Ⓐ darknes
- Ⓑ darkniss
- Ⓒ darkness
- Ⓓ darknis

14.
- Ⓔ gretness
- Ⓕ grateness
- Ⓖ greatness
- Ⓗ graitness

19.
- Ⓐ sickness
- Ⓑ sickniss
- Ⓒ sicknes
- Ⓓ siknes

5.
- Ⓐ producsion
- Ⓑ producton
- Ⓒ production
- Ⓓ priduction

10.
- Ⓔ encouragment
- Ⓕ encouragement
- Ⓖ encouragemint
- Ⓗ encuragement

15.
- Ⓐ intertaiment
- Ⓑ entertainment
- Ⓒ entertanment
- Ⓓ entertenement

20.
- Ⓔ goverment
- Ⓕ government
- Ⓖ governmnt
- Ⓗ govenmint

Words with Prefixes

Pretest Directions

Fold back the paper along the dotted line. Use the blanks to write each word as it is read aloud. When you finish the test, unfold the paper. Use the list at the right to correct any spelling mistakes. Practice the words you missed for the Posttest.

To Parents

Here are the results of your child's weekly spelling Pretest. You can help your child study for the Posttest by following these simple steps for each word on the word list:

1. Read the word to your child.

2. Have your child write the word, saying each letter as it is written.

3. Say each letter of the word as your child checks the spelling.

4. If a mistake has been made, have your child read each letter of the correctly spelled word aloud, and then repeat steps 1–3.

1. _____	1. redo
2. _____	2. unkind
3. _____	3. disappear
4. _____	4. reread
5. _____	5. nonfat
6. _____	6. inactive
7. _____	7. international
8. _____	8. unlucky
9. _____	9. dislike
10. _____	10. unpack
11. _____	11. nonstop
12. _____	12. refill
13. _____	13. uncertain
14. _____	14. interstate
15. _____	15. incomplete
16. _____	16. rewind
17. _____	17. unsure
18. _____	18. disagree
19. _____	19 reheat
20. _____	20. nonsense

Challenge Words

_____ identify

_____ mammals

_____ marine

_____ preserve

_____ related

Name_____ Date_____

Words with Prefixes

Using the Word Study Steps

1. LOOK at the word.

2. SAY the word aloud.

3. STUDY the letters in the word.

4. WRITE the word.

5. CHECK the word.

   Did you spell the word right?
   If not, go back to step 1.

> **Spelling Tip**
>
> Learn how to spell prefixes you use often in writing.
>
> *re-   un-   in-   dis-*
>
> *inter- non-*

X the Word

Put an X on the word that does NOT have the same prefix as the spelling word on the left.

1.	**redo**	return	red	2.	**reread**	retell	ready
3.	**refill**	rebuild	rental	4.	**reheat**	reach	refresh
5.	**unkind**	untold	under	6.	**unlucky**	unite	unfold
7.	**unpack**	unfold	uncle	8.	**uncertain**	uncover	unit

9. **incomplete**   ink   incurable

10. **inactive**   indirect   inch

11. **disappear**   disk   disrespect

12. **dislike**   dish   distrust

13. **international** interconnect intend

14. **nonfat**   none   nonviolent

15. **nonsense**   noon   nonstop

To Parents or Helpers

   Using the Word Study Steps above as your child comes across any new words will help him or her learn to spell words effectively. Review the steps as you both go over this week's spelling words.
   Go over the Spelling Tip with your child. Ask your child to spell the prefixes without looking at them.
   Help your child complete the spelling activity.

Words with Prefixes

redo	nonfat	dislike	uncertain	unsure
unkind	inactive	unpack	interstate	disagree
disappear	international	nonstop	incomplete	reheat
reread	unlucky	refill	rewind	nonsense

Pattern Power

Write the spelling words with the following prefixes.

words with *re-*

1. _____

2. _____

3. _____

4. _____

5. _____

words with *un-*

6. _____

7. _____

8. _____

9. _____

10. _____

words with *dis-*

11. _____

12. _____

13. _____

words with *inter-*

14. _____

15. _____

words with *in-*

16. _____

17. _____

words with *non-*

18. _____

19. _____

20. _____

Words with Prefixes

redo	nonfat	dislike	uncertain	unsure
unkind	inactive	unpack	interstate	disagree
disappear	international	nonstop	incomplete	reheat
reread	unlucky	refill	rewind	nonsense

Word Meaning: Prefixes

A prefix occurs at the beginning of a word. A prefix gives a word a different meaning. Read the meanings for the prefixes in your spelling words. Notice that *un-*, *dis-*, *in-*, and *non-* all share the meaning "the opposite of."

re-	"again"	*in-*	"not" or "the opposite of"
un-	"not" or "the opposite of"	*non-*	"without" or "the opposite of"
dis-	"not" or "the opposite of"	*inter-*	"between" or "among"

Write the spelling word that matches each meaning below.

1. do again _____

2. without fat _____

3. not active _____

4. between nations _____

5. without stopping _____

6. not lucky _____

7. opposite of like _____

8. fill again _____

9. not sure _____

10. heat again _____

Challenge Extension: Write one sentence for each of the Challenge Words. Read your sentences to a partner.

182

Grade 4/Unit 6
Whales 10

Words with Prefixes

Proofreading Activity

There are six spelling mistakes in the letter below. Circle the misspelled words. Write the words correctly on the lines below.

Dear Seth,

Last week I went whale watching. The humpback whales were so beautiful. It makes me so sad to think that one day whales may disapere. I think it is unkinde for people to hunt them. There is an internatunal law against killing whales. Some nations think whaling is not harmful, but I disagrea. Experts say that it is uncertin if all whale species will survive. In the past, whales have been unluky. Today, people all over the world are trying to save them.

1. _____   3. _____   5. _____

2. _____   4. _____   6. _____

Writing Activity

What animal would you like to protect? Write a few sentences about how that animal should be protected. Use four spelling words in your writing.

_____

_____

_____

_____

Words with Prefixes

Look at the words in each set below. One word in each set is spelled correctly. Use a pencil to fill in the circle next to the correct word. Before you begin, look at the sample sets of words. Sample A has been done for you. Do Sample B by yourself. When you are sure you know what to do, you may go on with the rest of the page.

Sample A
- Ⓐ reiruns
- Ⓑ reeruns
- Ⓒ rerunns
- ● reruns

Sample B
- Ⓔ untie
- Ⓕ untye
- Ⓖ intie
- Ⓗ unti

1.
- Ⓐ refil
- Ⓑ rifell
- Ⓒ refill
- Ⓓ rifill

6.
- Ⓔ unsure
- Ⓕ unsur
- Ⓖ unsuer
- Ⓗ unshur

11.
- Ⓐ nonfate
- Ⓑ nonefat
- Ⓒ nonfat
- Ⓓ nofat

16.
- Ⓔ imcomplete
- Ⓕ incompleat
- Ⓖ incomplete
- Ⓗ uncomplet

2.
- Ⓔ dislike
- Ⓕ disliek
- Ⓖ deslike
- Ⓗ disslike

7.
- Ⓐ riwend
- Ⓑ rewend
- Ⓒ rewind
- Ⓓ reewind

12.
- Ⓔ nonsense
- Ⓕ nonsesne
- Ⓖ nosense
- Ⓗ nonesense

17.
- Ⓐ reheet
- Ⓑ reaheat
- Ⓒ rehete
- Ⓓ reheat

3.
- Ⓐ enactive
- Ⓑ inactive
- Ⓒ inactiv
- Ⓓ inacitf

8.
- Ⓔ unpak
- Ⓕ unpac
- Ⓖ unpake
- Ⓗ unpack

13.
- Ⓐ enlucky
- Ⓑ unlucky
- Ⓒ unluky
- Ⓓ inlucky

18.
- Ⓔ incertain
- Ⓕ uncertain
- Ⓖ uncertin
- Ⓗ incertin

4.
- Ⓔ internationel
- Ⓕ interational
- Ⓖ international
- Ⓗ intunational

9.
- Ⓐ disapear
- Ⓑ disappear
- Ⓒ disapere
- Ⓓ desappear

14.
- Ⓔ redo
- Ⓕ redoe
- Ⓖ reedo
- Ⓗ reddo

19.
- Ⓐ rereed
- Ⓑ reread
- Ⓒ rerede
- Ⓓ reeread

5.
- Ⓐ nunstop
- Ⓑ nonstop
- Ⓒ nostop
- Ⓓ nonstep

10.
- Ⓔ interstate
- Ⓕ intersate
- Ⓖ inerstate
- Ⓗ intastate

15.
- Ⓐ uncind
- Ⓑ unkind
- Ⓒ unkinnd
- Ⓓ inkind

20.
- Ⓔ disaggre
- Ⓕ desagree
- Ⓖ disagree
- Ⓗ disagre

Words from Math

Pretest Directions

Fold back the paper along the dotted line. Use the blanks to write each word as it is read aloud. When you finish the test, unfold the paper. Use the list at the right to correct any spelling mistakes. Practice the words you missed for the Posttest.

To Parents

Here are the results of your child's weekly spelling Pretest. You can help your child study for the Posttest by following these simple steps for each word on the word list:

1. Read the word to your child.

2. Have your child write the word, saying each letter as it is written.

3. Say each letter of the word as your child checks the spelling.

4. If a mistake has been made, have your child read each letter of the correctly spelled word aloud, and then repeat steps 1–3.

1. _____	1. area
2. _____	2. hundreds
3. _____	3. size
4. _____	4. billions
5. _____	5. weight
6. _____	6. minute
7. _____	7. noon
8. _____	8. cone
9. _____	9. yard
10. _____	10. edge
11. _____	11. amount
12. _____	12. cylinder
13. _____	13. zero
14. _____	14. figure
15. _____	15. calendar
16. _____	16. quart
17. _____	17. decade
18. _____	18. rectangle
19. _____	19 era
20. _____	20. length

Challenge Words

_____ compares

_____ importance

_____ instance

_____ lurk

_____ soggy

Name_____ Date_____

Words from Math

Using the Word Study Steps

1. LOOK at the word.
2. SAY the word aloud.
3. STUDY the letters in the word.
4. WRITE the word.
5. CHECK the word.

   Did you spell the word right?
   If not, go back to step 1.

Spelling Tip
Become familiar with the dictionary and use it often.

Find Rhyming Words

Circle the word in each row that rhymes with the spelling word on the left.

1. **quart**	short	quick	quail
2. **yard**	yield	hard	board
3. **noon**	none	one	balloon
4. **weight**	though	week	date
5. **size**	maze	rise	breeze
6. **length**	enough	eighth	strength
7. **cone**	soon	none	bone
8. **amount**	among	count	about
9. **edge**	ledge	egg	badge
10. **zero**	cow	hero	true

To Parents or Helpers

Using the Word Study Steps above as your child comes across any new words will help him or her learn to spell words effectively. Review the steps as you both go over this week's spelling words.

Help your child look up other math words, and words from other subjects, in a dictionary.

Help your child complete the rhyming activity.

Words from Math

area	weight	yard	zero	decade
hundreds	minute	edge	figure	rectangle
size	noon	amount	calendar	era
billions	cone	cylinder	quart	length

Write the spelling words that tell about:

Numbers

1. _____

2. _____

3. _____

4. _____

Shapes

5. _____

6. _____

7. _____

8. _____

9. _____

10. _____

11. _____

Time

12. _____

13. _____

14. _____

15. _____

16. _____

Measurement

17. _____

18. _____

19. _____

20. _____

Write the spelling words *quart*, *cylinder*, *zero*, and *hundreds* in alphabetical order.

21. _____

22. _____

23. _____

24. _____

Words from Math

area	weight	yard	zero	decade
hundreds	minute	edge	figure	rectangle
size	noon	amount	calendar	era
billions	cone	cylinder	quart	length

What is the Meaning?

Write the spelling word that belongs in each group.

1. triangle, _____

2. tens, _____

3. millions, _____

4. _____, hour

5. _____, midnight

6. year, _____

7. foot, _____

8. pint, _____

What's the Word?

Complete each sentence with a spelling word.

9. The playground is that whole _____ behind the school.

10. If you subtract four from four, you'll end up with _____.

11. What _____ shoes do you wear?

12. We circled her birthday on the _____.

13. Move the cup away from the _____ of the table.

14. What _____ of money do you need to buy the car?

15. A three-sided _____ is called a triangle.

16. The _____ of the hallway is about 50 feet.

17. The _____ in which dinosaurs lived was long ago.

18. I have gained a lot of _____ from eating cookies.

Words from Math

Proofreading Activity

There are six spelling mistakes in the paragraph below. Circle the misspelled words. Write the words correctly on the lines below.

> The Everglades covers an areah of about 5,000 square miles in southern Florida. Its siz makes it one of the largest wetlands in the world. During the past decad a growing population and farming has harmed this wetland. Today, alligators must be protected or they will die out. An alligator's lenth can measure 9 feet or more. Their wayt can be as much as 250 pounds. If we do not save the Everglades, the erah of the Florida alligator may be over.

1. _____   3. _____   5. _____

2. _____   4. _____   6. _____

Writing Activity

Write about an animal or a place that you would like to save. Use four spelling words in your writing.

_____

_____

_____

_____

Words from Math

Look at the words in each set below. One word in each set is spelled correctly. Use a pencil to fill in the circle next to the correct word. Before you begin, look at the sample sets of words. Sample A has been done for you. Do Sample B by yourself. When you are sure you know what to do, you may go on with the rest of the page.

Sample A
- Ⓐ foote
- Ⓑ fut
- Ⓒ foot
- Ⓓ fute

Sample B
- Ⓔ intch
- Ⓕ inch
- Ⓖ inche
- Ⓗ insh

1.
- Ⓐ aree
- Ⓑ areu
- Ⓒ arae
- Ⓓ area

2.
- Ⓔ hundredz
- Ⓕ hundreds
- Ⓖ hundrids
- Ⓗ hungdreds

3.
- Ⓐ sise
- Ⓑ siz
- Ⓒ size
- Ⓓ siez

4.
- Ⓔ billions
- Ⓕ bilionz
- Ⓖ billionz
- Ⓗ bilyuns

5.
- Ⓐ wate
- Ⓑ weite
- Ⓒ weight
- Ⓓ weiht

6.
- Ⓔ minut
- Ⓕ minit
- Ⓖ minite
- Ⓗ minute

7.
- Ⓐ nume
- Ⓑ noon
- Ⓒ nyon
- Ⓓ noen

8.
- Ⓔ conne
- Ⓕ coen
- Ⓖ cone
- Ⓗ coan

9.
- Ⓐ yerd
- Ⓑ yard
- Ⓒ yarde
- Ⓓ yord

10.
- Ⓔ edje
- Ⓕ edg
- Ⓖ edge
- Ⓗ edj

11.
- Ⓐ umount
- Ⓑ umownt
- Ⓒ amownt
- Ⓓ amount

12.
- Ⓔ cylinder
- Ⓕ cilinder
- Ⓖ cilunder
- Ⓗ cylander

13.
- Ⓐ zeero
- Ⓑ zero
- Ⓒ ziro
- Ⓓ zeiro

14.
- Ⓔ fighure
- Ⓕ figgure
- Ⓖ figyure
- Ⓗ figure

15.
- Ⓐ calunder
- Ⓑ callendar
- Ⓒ calendar
- Ⓓ callindar

16.
- Ⓔ qwart
- Ⓕ quart
- Ⓖ quert
- Ⓗ quarte

17.
- Ⓐ decad
- Ⓑ deceide
- Ⓒ decade
- Ⓓ deckade

18.
- Ⓔ rectangle
- Ⓕ recktangle
- Ⓖ recktangl
- Ⓗ rectangel

19.
- Ⓐ eera
- Ⓑ era
- Ⓒ eru
- Ⓓ erah

20.
- Ⓔ linght
- Ⓕ lenth
- Ⓖ lengtch
- Ⓗ length

Grade 4/Unit 6 Review Test

Read each sentence. If an underlined word is spelled wrong, fill in the circle that goes with that word. If no word is spelled wrong, fill in the circle below NONE. Read Sample A, and do Sample B.

A. Can you <u>recut</u> my <u>hare</u> <u>tonight</u>?
        A   B   C

                             NONE
A. Ⓐ ⬤ Ⓒ Ⓓ

B. I <u>caught</u> the <u>bear</u> eating from a <u>bowl</u>.
      E   F   G

                             NONE
B. Ⓔ Ⓕ Ⓖ Ⓗ

1. <u>Bury</u> or <u>need</u> the <u>dates</u> into the bread dough.
    A   B   C

                             NONE
1. Ⓐ Ⓑ Ⓒ Ⓓ

2. His <u>weight</u> was so <u>grate</u>, his feet became <u>numb</u>.
       E   F   G

                             NONE
2. Ⓔ Ⓕ Ⓖ Ⓗ

3. I need <u>encouragemint</u> to be <u>calm</u> in <u>darkness</u>.
           A   B   C

                             NONE
3. Ⓐ Ⓑ Ⓒ Ⓓ

4. <u>Hundreds</u> of bubbles give babies <u>nonstop</u> <u>delite</u>.
    E   F   G

                             NONE
4. Ⓔ Ⓕ Ⓖ Ⓗ

5. I am <u>unsure</u> that the car <u>cylinder</u> caused the <u>reck</u>.
         A   B   C

                             NONE
5. Ⓐ Ⓑ Ⓒ Ⓓ

6. <u>Grate</u> cheese and chop <u>dates</u> for <u>great</u> flavor.
    E   F   G

                             NONE
6. Ⓔ Ⓕ Ⓖ Ⓗ

7. A <u>nonstop</u> ride in <u>darknes</u> left us <u>breathless</u>.
        A   B   C

                             NONE
7. Ⓐ Ⓑ Ⓒ Ⓓ

8. For your <u>protecshun</u>, <u>rewind</u> the <u>adjustable</u> alarm.
            E   F   G

                             NONE
8. Ⓔ Ⓕ Ⓖ Ⓗ

9. I <u>disagree</u> that <u>inactive</u> volcanoes are <u>bilions</u> of years old.
        A   B   C

                             NONE
9. Ⓐ Ⓑ Ⓒ Ⓓ

10. It <u>dates</u> back to an <u>era</u> <u>hundeds</u> of years ago.
      E   F   G

                             NONE
10. Ⓔ Ⓕ Ⓖ Ⓗ

11. Without <u>encouragement</u>, I became <u>numb</u> and <u>unsure</u>.
             A   B   C

                             NONE
11. Ⓐ Ⓑ Ⓒ Ⓓ

Grade 4 Unit 6 Review Test

12. Make a <u>great</u> <u>bury</u> pie. <u>Knead</u> the dough first!   12. Ⓔ Ⓕ Ⓖ NONE Ⓗ
           E   F   G

13. He became <u>inactive</u> and lost <u>wait</u> after a train <u>wreck</u>.   13. Ⓐ Ⓑ Ⓒ NONE Ⓓ
              A   B   C

14. I am <u>breathless</u> with <u>delight</u> to be a part of this <u>era</u>.   14. Ⓔ Ⓕ Ⓖ NONE Ⓗ
           E   F   G

15. For <u>protection</u> from fire, <u>bury</u> the <u>cylinder</u> of gas.   15. Ⓐ Ⓑ Ⓒ NONE Ⓓ
         A   B   C

16. "<u>Grate</u> <u>billions</u> of cabbages <u>nostop</u>," I said.   16. Ⓔ Ⓕ Ⓖ NONE Ⓗ
       E   F   G

17. I <u>disagre</u> that <u>berry</u> pie makes me gain <u>weight</u>.   17. Ⓐ Ⓑ Ⓒ NONE Ⓓ
        A   B   C

18. <u>Billions</u> of stars in the sky keep me <u>cam</u> in the <u>darkness</u>. 18. Ⓔ Ⓕ Ⓖ NONE Ⓗ
     E   F   G

19. <u>Encouragement</u> and <u>protection</u> make a baby <u>calm</u>.   19. Ⓐ Ⓑ Ⓒ NONE Ⓓ
       A   B   C

20. I'm <u>unshure</u> about the <u>hundreds</u> of <u>adjustable</u> chairs.   20. Ⓔ Ⓕ Ⓖ NONE Ⓗ
      E   F   G

21. <u>Rewind</u> the <u>enactive</u> toys to <u>delight</u> the children.   21. Ⓐ Ⓑ Ⓒ NONE Ⓓ
    A   B   C

22. Seeing her <u>berry</u> the gold left me <u>breathless</u> and <u>numb</u>. 22. Ⓔ Ⓕ Ⓖ NONE Ⓗ
         E   F   G

23. We measured the <u>berry</u> in an <u>adjustabel</u> <u>cylinder</u>.   23. Ⓐ Ⓑ Ⓒ NONE Ⓓ
         A   B   C

24. In which <u>ira</u> did humans first <u>knead</u> and <u>grate</u> foods?   24. Ⓔ Ⓕ Ⓖ NONE Ⓗ
       E   F   G

25. I <u>disagree</u> that the toy will <u>wreck</u> if you <u>rewined</u> it.   25. Ⓐ Ⓑ Ⓒ NONE Ⓓ
    A   B   C